WILLIAM KNIBB:

MISSIONARY IN JAMAICA

A MEMOIR

BY

Mrs. JOHN JAMES SMITH.

WITH AN INTRODUCTION BY

REV. J. G. GREENHOUGH, M A.

"Is not this the fast that I have chosen? to loose the bands of wickedness, to undo
the heavy burdens, and to let the oppressed go free, and that ye break
every yoke?"

London:

ALEXANDER & SHEPHEARD, FURNIVAL STREET, E.C

1896.

PREFACE.

SINCE the proof sheets of this little book have come from the printer the writer's attention has been called to the funeral sermon preached by the Rev. John Aldis in Maze Pond Chapel on the occasion of Mr. Knibb's death (November, 1845). A few sentences quoted from it will, perhaps, form a better preface than any other.

"A little more than one-and-twenty years ago you might have seen a young man, accompanied by his wife, going on board a ship. He leaves for a distant island, to be a schoolmaster, perhaps an assistant preacher of the Gospel, to ignorant and wretched slaves. A few friends attend him, who regret his departure, and hope he may be useful in the humblest rank of missionary labourers. At home, a widowed mother commends him to GOD, saying in spirit, 'I had rather he died on his passage than disgrace religion.' To his countrymen his enterprise is unknown or contemptible. Of his own denomination but few have ever heard his name. Unknown, uncared for, he departs unnoticed, as the single leaf falls in the forest. A few weeks ago he was carried to his grave. Wise and good men, from the distance of many miles, were gathered to that solemnity. Ministers of different denominations officiated at it. Magistrates, men of wealth and station, were there as mourning a public calamity. Eight thousand of the grateful poor hung about that procession. A deep, unutterable grief saddened every countenance and swelled every heart. The proud were humble, the noisy quiet, the malignant kind. One spell-word bound them all: 'He is dead!' There is much in the interval between that voyage and that funeral.

"The true leader not only has an intuitive sagacity to discover the right way, and the promptitude and courage to advance in it, but the strange power of fascination, which draws others after him.

"This is the honour we claim for our departed friend; or, rather, this is the grace which we conceive our GOD conferred upon him. ` He was a leader, and a great one."

Not that Mr. Knibb was alone in the work. Among his brother missionaries he worked shoulder to shoulder, but here in England he was often their spokesman, and had the power to make his story tell. So he was the most widely-known and the recognised leader of the movement.

William Knibb "had good tidings of great joy" for those who walked in darkness—"the glorious Gospel of the blessed God."

The poor people of Jamaica received the message, many of them, with joy, but as children needing constant guidance, and very dependent on the missionary. It was his earnest desire and constant effort that these babes in Christ should grow to the stature of a "perfect man in Christ Jesus;" and that for all the coloured peasantry a good primary education should be provided, such as would help them to gain an honest livelihood, not only as labourers earning fair wages, but with opportunity, such as had it in them, to rise, and there were many capable of this. And if they maintained themselves they were also to feel the responsibility of maintaining their pastors, educated pastors, and of contributing towards sending to others the Gospel they valued themselves.

The struggle was hard, both to obtain freedom and to live through troublous years following, when, from various circumstances, the times, in our West Indian colonies, were so bad that some people began to doubt the expediency of emancipation, but the good fruit has ripened now, and the desires of William Knibb have largely come to pass. Nor his desires alone. William Carey, the wonderful leader of the modern missionary movement, prayed as well "for the slaves as for the heathen." Carey went, that being the path opened to him, to the heathen, but God answered *both* his prayers.

The first thought of writing another account of William Knibb had its birth in the centenary year of the Baptist Mission. Not a word too much was said about Carey, but some of those who remember the Jubilee meetings at Kettering knew that Mr. Knibb, a Kettering man, had been on that occasion the centre of interest. It seemed a sad thing that one who had done so much for the sons of Africa should pass in any degree out of memory.

It has been difficult not to say more of co-adjutors, but it has been thought wise to kee_

this effort in so small a compass as to concentrate
the attention on Mr. Knibb, who went through,
and led others through, all the struggle.

Thanks are due and heartily given to the Rev.
John Brown Myers for much valuable assistance;
to the Rev. Ellis Fray for the loan of his grand-
father's letters; and to the Rev. D. J. East for
allowing the use of original documents about the
troubled times of 1832, notably the MS. journal
of the Rev. W. Dendy, who arrived just in the
worst of the disturbance. It may be stated that
the form admitting the missionaries to bail and
the subsequent letter setting them free, no charges
having been found against them, are both in
Mr. East's possession.

M. E. S.

CONTENTS.

CHAPTER VI.

CHAPTER VII.

CHAPTER VIII.

CHAPTER IX.

CHAPTER X.

CHAPTER XI.

LIST OF ILLUSTRATIONS.

INTRODUCTION.

JAMAICA has changed little in its external features
since the memorable days which are treated of in
the following pages. There has been no rapid
march of civilisation and commerce converting
sea-board hamlets into grimy ports, and sylvan
scenes into dense masses of smoke-charged
ugliness. The country is as rural and as
lovely as when Knibb saw it, and there are few
signs of the engineer save in the somewhat
scanty but well-kept highways and in the narrow
railroad which threads its course across the
island so deeply imbedded in rich vegetation
that it cannot in any degree mar the beauty in
which it is hidden.

The population, however, has increased from
about 400,000 to nearly 650,000, and is composed
of white and coloured people. The former number
only about 15,000 of the whole, and the latter
call themselves, by way of distinction, "the
people."

Much the same may be said of some of the
towns. Kingston, it is true, presents a considerably different aspect. A wide, sandy area in the
centre of the city has been converted into an
ornamental public garden; the streets are now

lighted with gas, and nearly all the public buildings, churches, and chapels with electric luminants. The wharfage has been largely extended for the accommodation of Atlantic and coasting steamers, which have largely supplanted sailing ships.

But Old Spanish Town, with its massive public buildings, relics of ancient dignity, preserves in semi-slumber a sort of decayed gentility, and makes one wonder how the people in it live. Falmouth, too, with its spacious market-place, its quaint buildings, its military barracks, its malarious marsh-land, its ubiquitous mosquitoes, and its doctoring sea-breezes, has just the old face unchanged which Knibb knew and loved so well. And Montego Bay, where some of the leading and most tragical parts of his life were played, still nestles semi-circled on the hill slopes, looking down on a sea of marvellous beauty, with hardly an added feature or building with which he would not be familiar. But a line of steamers now runs between this port and New York; and Port Antonio vies with it by another line, especially in its fruit trade.

The occupation and industries of the people are not quite as they were. The sugar-growing, which was formerly the main source of wealth, is now not of principal importance. One sees, indeed, acres and acres of the sugar-cane which was once so famous, and here and there, in the midst, a factory, but the product of this is

not simply the innocent article which serves for
the sweetening of tea, but the far stronger
article which is known as Jamaica rum. One
catches the pungent flavour of it in all parts of
the island, and is agreeably and thankfully
surprised to find that with this alcoholic com-
modity everywhere plentiful and cheap, there is
comparatively little excess in drinking among
the negroes. But fruit growing now forms a
continually increasing item in the business and
exports of the island, and a large number of
tropical products, such as spices and dye woods,
have been added to that which had once almost a
monopoly.

In many parts, and particularly on the higher
levels, the land is cultivated by small freeholders,
who, with their three or four acres of bananas,
oranges, yams, and prolific mangoes, manage to
maintain themselves and families and to have a
little to spare. They live in a very simple and
somewhat rude style, but all their necessary wants
are supplied, and they are very proud of the inde-
pendence which they have gained. Some of our
most vigorous churches in the island are found
where these men and their households form the
bulk of the membership. The wages paid for field
labour by the larger landowners are so small—not
much, if any more, than a shilling a day, that one
is hardly surprised to find the people reluctant to
undertake it if they can turn to anything which is
easier or more remunerative. They prefer naturally

to be their own masters, and work a little plot of
their own, if it is by any means procurable ; and it
may be that from this cause has arisen the complaint
which the planters are constantly making about
the laziness of the negroes. But certainly, if any
trustworthy conclusion could be drawn from a
hurried visit, and what one sees in the course of it,
I should not say they are exceptionally addicted
to that particular vice. I saw hundreds of them,
toiling early and late, under the scorching sun,
in a way of which no British labourer would be
ashamed. But, for the most part, they were working on their own land, which makes all the
difference.

In the matter of carrying and fetching, however,
the male member of the negro community has still
a few needed lessons to learn. He seems to think
that his work is done when the product is ready
for market, and lays upon his wife the burden of
conveying it thither; and many a time one's
patience is a little tried, and a feeling of disgust
slightly provoked, by seeing the husband on horse-
back entirely unencumbered, while his gentle
partner trudges wearily at his side for miles,
bowed down under a load of fifty or sixty pounds
weight. She takes it cheerfully enough, and so
does he, naturally; but an Englishman, who looks
upon this unequal division of labour with perhaps
prejudiced eyes, is tempted to revile. This, no
doubt, is a relic of long-established habit dating
from slavery times.

Those days are not quite forgotten. One meets with very old men who remember vividly the sadness and the cruelty and the horrors of them, and find a mournful pleasure in going over the dark recital. Very dear to these old men are the names of those heroic missionaries who stood up for the oppressed in those evil times, and hardly less dear to the middle-aged men, who received the story direct from their suffering fathers. In Falmouth, and all around the district, the mention of Knibb's name brings tears. At Montego Bay and Mount Carey, Knibb is recalled with profound feeling, but Burchell's is the name held in greatest reverence; while at Spanish Town and in the south of the island there is no word so potent as Phillippo.

But the young generation know slavery only as a fading tradition, a thing of the past with which they have but a remote historical connection. They do not like to be reminded of it, and told that their grandsires were bought and sold like chattels. They have an unquestionable pride, which endeavours, as much as possible, to ignore that humiliation, and, in speaking to them, one soon learns the wisdom of touching lightly, 'if at all, on those ancient facts. They are glad to be spoken of as free-born subjects of the Queen. The people, both young and old in fact, but the young especially, are British in sentiment though African by race. They are proud of the empire of which they

form part. The geography of the British Isles
and of the empire is taught in all the
Elementary schools, and the young people
acquire fair knowledge of it; and young
and old are passionately loyal to the Queen.
No assembly in our own land would sing the
National Anthem more enthusiastically than one
hears it in the gatherings of Jamaica people.

The people have made great advance in both
mental and moral qualities since they were
delivered from the degrading bondage by which
body and mind were chained down and aspiration
crushed. The educational system, generously
supported by Government, is now well nigh
universal, and at least brings elementary instruction within the reach of all. There is, I think,
no compulsory attendance, but the strong sentiment in favour of education, and the laudable
ambition of the people to have their children raised
in social status, produce the same or better results
than compulsion. One meets with a considerable
number of older persons who are unable to read
and write, but very few of the younger men and
women, and in a comparatively short time the
illiterate class will have practically ceased to
exist.

These pages show the profound interest which
Knibb took in the matter of education and the
establishment of schools. His far-seeing and
statesman-like mind, while earnestly engaged in
the urgent demands of the moment, was ever busy

laying wise plans for the future. He saw that if the people were to be really elevated and free, and the churches intelligent and self-supporting, secular teaching must go hand in hand with the religious work. The happy results of his foresight are everywhere apparent. Nearly all our churches have their schoolhouse and schoolmaster, which, with the help of the Government grant, are sustained by the free-will offerings of the people; and my visits to these schools brought me to the conclusion that the children are nearly as well taught as, and perhaps more eager to learn than, the children in our Board schools at home.

Knibb was equally solicitous about the training of a native ministry which should gradually take the place of the European missionary, and the institution of Calabar College was largely due to his efforts. In that institution there are now between thirty and forty students, two-thirds of whom are being trained as schoolmasters, and the rest for ministerial work. They are young men of intelligence and fervent spirit, and in general ability and culture compare not unfavourably with the students in our home colleges. The general maintenance and management of the college are a charge upon the Jamaica churches, save that the tutors receive their stipends from the Home Society.

This is the last remaining burden on the funds of that Society, the religious work being in all other respects self-supporting, and we may well regard that expenditure without distrust when we consider the admirable part which the college is taking in supplying the religious needs of the island. The men trained in it are gradually displacing the white minister. Two-thirds of the churches are now happily shepherded by men of their own colour, and this proportion is continually increasing. The white ministers are greatly loved and honoured, and they are in nearly every instance men whose fine spirit, temper, and culture would command respect anywhere. The Jamaica negroes are rapidly acquiring self-respect. There is great pride of race, self-dependence, belief in themselves and in the capabilities of their people. And there is so much of latent energy and promise in this feeling that it is welcome to everyone who takes a large and generous view of their future.

While the people are steadily growing in intelligence they seem to have made more rapid strides in morality and religion. When it is remembered that emancipation found them in an almost sickening moral degradation, with no clear notion of even the elementary virtues, with the sexual relations depraved, with habits long established of dishonesty and untruthfulness, it is almost surprising, and truly gratifying, to observe the change for the better which has been wrought. The members of our churches especially are in many respects as exemplary in conduct and character as the average professor at home. Large numbers of them, especially of the young people, are total abstainers, and sobriety is so well-established among them that cases of church discipline in which intemperance is involved are exceedingly rare. If in any one respect they compare unfavourably with the home churches, it is in the greater frequency with which the sin of unchastity has to be dealt with, though in this particular there is a continual advance towards better things.

In religious feeling they show all the finer qualities of the negro race. Their emotions are easily stirred and easily wrought into enthusiasm ; their fervour is genuine and deep, and, as long experience has proved, well sustained. Their delight in all religious exercises is unmistakable ; and their joy in the Lord, and in their appreciation of His undeserved grace, is enough to provoke a sense of shame in colder natures, and to bring tears to the eyes of those who are more sensitive. Altogether, the religious element is more to them than it is to the majority of our own people—more in the sense that it occupies a larger proportionate space in their regards, and enters more largely into their every-day thoughts.

One of the most welcome features in their Church life is the part which youth has in it. Most of the candidates for baptism are of an early age, and nearly one-third of those who keep the Feast of Remembrance at the Lord's Table are young men and women. Equally gratifying is the interest which all alike take in the spread of the Gospel through the heathen world. Their missionary meetings are seasons of profound interest and unbounded fervour. They have a missionary society of their own which carries on evangelising work in those neighbouring islands, where the people of their own race are either in heathen darkness, or in the darkness—well-nigh as dense— of Romanism in its most superstitious and degraded form. And the fact that they contribute more than two thousand pounds out of their very poverty for this work is one of the most striking testimonies that could be given to the depth and earnestness of their religious thoughts.

The Baptist Churches have held their ground well through all these years, and slowly increased their membership, but it was not to be expected, nor was it possible indeed, that the rapid growth and extension which the early days of the mission witnessed could be continued.

The statistics of our churches show a membership of about 37,000, and if to these are added all those, not church members, who are more or less associated with them in worship, they may be said to embrace nearly one-fifth of the entire population. They stand first in number among the religious bodies. The Episcopal Church comes next and

then the Wesleyans, while the Independents and
Presbyterians have a smaller but not insignificant
place.   Altogether the island is pre-eminently
Christian, the number of habitual church-goers
being far greater in proportion than we are able to
boast of in our own favoured land.

The course of the narrative in the ensuing pages
shows, in pathetic and sympathetic lines, the sufferings and trials in which the work was begun and
carried on—a work which has yielded such large
and abiding results.   Very literally the people
" received the word in much affliction with joy
of the Holy Ghost."   The missionary was opposed
and reviled, and his hearers threatened and
terrorised and spitefully used at every step, but all
these things eventually worked together for good.
For, not to speak of the patience and splendid
heroism which were developed in the missionaries
by their rough and often tragical experience,
there was another outcome of the persecution
which no policy could have foreseen or planned,
and which favoured immensely the progress of
the work.

The fact that the missionary's presence was
resented, and he himself suspected and hated by
the white planters, and, indeed, the whole white
colony on the island, forced him to throw in his
lot entirely with the suffering coloured population
whom he had come to evangelise.   He could not
make his home and friendships or even visiting
acquaintances among the higher class people of

his own race. There was no temptation to dwell
among them, or in any way to prefer their society.
That which the missionary commonly and almost
inevitably does in India, was made impossible in
Jamaica by the incidents of the position. He was
practically ostracised from white society, and all
his sympathies and interests were engaged on the
side of the oppressed negroes. He championed
their cause, defended their rights, pleaded on
behalf of their wrongs, had his house built among
them, shared many of their privations, treated
them as equals and brothers, and was everywhere
regarded as a father and friend. From the first
he won their trust and tearful gratitude, and
they responded with hearts full of love and eagerly
open to his message. The Gospel was presented
to them in its most attractive and persuasive form,
in lives that were embodiments of Christian compassion, self-denial, and sweet brotherhood, and
they embraced it with all the swift fervour and
emotion of their nature.

The close and tender relationship which was
thus established between the missionary and his
convert remains, to a large extent, to the present
time in the happy, trustful bonds which bind pastor
and Church together. The reverence and love in
which the people hold their minister are most
touching and impressive. His influence among
them is almost beyond computation. He might
exercise all the authority of a priest if his
principles did not forbid it. His word is almost

sacred, and his counsel implicitly followed. As in the former days, so still, to a great degree, they go to him for help and advice in all difficulties. In many districts he is the lawyer to whom they refer all disputes, the doctor whose help they seek in sickness, the father whose direction they ask in questions of marriage, and the friend to whom they carry all their hearts' troubles. Every day and almost every hour he seems to be at their service, and his house is never long without its applicant for some guiding and kindly word. At morning and evening prayers there is often a small congregation—those of the people who dwell near or are working in the neighbouring fields steal in one by one at the appointed time to follow the reading and join in the prayer, and sing with the utmost heartiness the sweet familiar hymn, and then, after a respectful and loving greeting, quietly depart.

"Blessed are the people who know the joyful sound," and blessed were the feet of those who first brought to them this sound. Nowhere is there a finer demonstration of the power of the Gospel, or a nobler vindication of missionary effort than is furnished in Jamaica. The sufferings of .Knibb and his co-labourers have been fruitful beyond measure. If one may quote without irreverence words which were spoken of the Highest, we might say of these heroic pioneers, "They shall see of the travail of their soul and be satisfied." Great was their toil, magnificent their faith and courage, and great is the harvest which has been reaped from their labours. There is an inspiration in the story of their lives, and an incentive to patient hope in the results of their sanctified energies. Truly "they rest from their labours, and their works do follow them."

J. G. GREENHOUGH.

WILLIAM KNIBB.

CHAPTER I.

EARLY DAYS.

WITH his heart full of the great enterprise which he had as yet no power of carrying out, Carey prayed in private and in public for the "*slaves* and the heathens."

In 1793, he himself went to the heathen, our first modern English missionary. How shall his prayer for the *slaves* be fulfilled?

As there were reformers before the Reformation, so there was evangelical teaching before the system of modern missions began. In the West Indies the Moravians were the pioneers, as in some other parts of the world. They went to Jamaica in 1754. Later, the Methodists did some good work, but before they arrived came the first Baptist preacher—a coloured man from America—named George Leile. His master had left him his freedom by will, and he came to Kingston and set up in business as a carrier.

NOTE.—A tradition has been handed down amongst the people of the Manchester Mountains, Jamaica, that many years ago a free black man visited the neighbourhood; that he talked to the slaves about Jesus, and afterwards baptized some of them. At length, on one of his preaching excursions, he was seized by the opponents of the Gospel and hung. If this is true, Jamaica has had her proto-martyr.—*See* "Voice of Jubilee," p. 37.

Having been the pastor of a coloured congregation in Georgia, he soon began work among the West Indian negroes.

He had his share of persecution, being put in prison on a charge of sedition, of which he was acquitted, and also had the misfortune, having made himself responsible for the arrears due on his chapel, of being imprisoned for debt.

The people who gathered round Leile in Kingston formed little knots among themselves when they moved away. They were very ignorant. Old superstitions and the old moral code soon mixed themselves up with the recollection, ever growing fainter, of Christian doctrine, so that when the English missionaries came, they found them for the most part in need of much further training before they could be consistent Church members. In fact, these negroes held aloof in general from the European pastors.

It was, however, from one of Leile's followers that the call, "Come over and help us," came. A certain Mr. Wynn having bought some of Mr. Leile's people, discovered that they were much distressed for want of their religious services. He must have been a kind master, for, finding them unhappy, he engaged Moses Baker, one of Leile's people, to come and teach them.

Moses Baker, good but illiterate, when he found age creeping over him, had wisdom enough to apply for help to Dr. Ryland. (One wonders how he knew there was such a person.) Here was the opening Dr Ryland had desired. It reanimated a long-cherished feeling, and gave it a practical direction. "I have waited," he says, "for several years with great anxiety for some one to send." The first missionary sent out was John Rowe, of Yeovil, Somersetshire. He arrived in Jamaica February 7th, 1814.

The sixth name on the list of missionaries is that of Thomas Knibb; of those who preceded him the best

WILLIAM KNIBB'S BIRTHPLACE.

remembered names were James Coultart and Joshua Tinson.

Thomas Knibb was born in 1791; his brother William in 1803; the latter ten years after Carey's departure for India, Kettering, the very town where the Baptist Missionary Society was formed, being the birthplace of both.

Thomas learnt with avidity, and was recommended, when old enough, by his teacher to Mr. J. G. Fuller, son of Carey's staunch friend and co-worker, who brought him into his printing-office, and on his removal to Bristol took the lad with him. Thomas begged that his brother William might go too : William, the good-natured, popular, vivacious boy, governed by his affections, but hardly to be controlled in any other way. He had, however, according to Mr. Fuller, already, at thirteen, developed the Carey-like trait of a resolute, unbending pursuit of everything he undertook.

After a while both brothers were persuaded to teach in the Sunday-school. The question soon came home to William, how he could urge upon the boys that religion was of vital importance, unless he were a Christian himself. In this state of mind an address given by his master, Mr. Fuller, was used by God's Spirit to bring him to a decision.

On the 7th of March, 1822, he was baptized by Dr. Ryland, who had baptized Carey thirty-nine years before—another point of touch with the pioneers of the Mission.

In the same year Thomas Knibb was designated by the Baptist Missionary Society for Jamaica. Missionary work was no new idea to him. His first thought had been drawn to it while he was putting in type the periodical accounts of the mission for Mr. Fuller. Those of us who are accustomed, at this end of the century, to the constant appeal for more missionaries, will read with curious interest the following quotation from Mr. Thomas Knibb's address on the occasion of his designation :—

"Towards the end of 1815, while conversing on the subject of missionary work with Mr. Fuller, he asked me whether I should like to go, and intimated, at the same time, that should native preachers speedily be raised up, European missionaries would not be required. I could not help secretly wishing that all the posts of missions might not be filled up till I was old enough to go "

He was sixteen at the time of this conversation, and sadly troubled lest he should grow up too late to be of use

William by this time was longing for the same work, but not troubled by the same fear. Always hopeful, he comforted his brother by saying, " Never mind, Thomas, the Society cannot do without printers, and I am sure Mr. Fuller will recommend us, and then we can preach, too, if we like."

The desire for usefulness abroad showed its healthy character by leading William to such channels of usefulness at home as he could enter.

"Andrew first findeth his own brother Simon and brought him to Jesus," William Knibb wrote, a few weeks after his baptism, to his brother James and to his sister Fanny ; his twin sister Ann was also given to his prayers and efforts on her behalf. At Bristol his activities widened from the Broadmead Sunday-school to a village station at Stapleton, two miles off, and deepened into the dark under-life of Brick Lane, where a blind man, a member of the church at Broadmead, had instituted a mission.

His congregation at Brick Lane rose in twelve months from about ten persons to sixty. Brick Lane led to Beggar's Opera, or Beggar's Uproars, as it came to be called, not without appreciation of the fitness of things. Here he would find men carousing, and it is said that "when he spoke to them they at once became still and hearkened to him with great attention." The Uproars was a place into which few people would have ventured, and in which far fewer would have been listened to.

Thomas Knibb landed in Jamaica on the 20th of January, 1823. He wrote home a glowing account of his first Sunday on the island, and gave some hope that an opening might be made for William The following is an extract from William's answer :—

"I refer to the question which you propounded in your last, and wished me to state my views respecting it.

"But what, my dear brother, what shall I say? How shall I reply? Oh, I do earnestly implore the guidance and assistance of the Holy Spirit to enable me to decide aright, and I can truly say that I have made, and do still make, it a matter of earnest prayer to be guided by unerring wisdom ! My prayer is, that, if it be consistent with the glory of God I should go, He would open a way; but if not, that I may never leave the British shores.

"For some time before you left Bristol, or I had any thought that you would go to Jamaica, 1 felt an earnest desire to be employed in teaching the poor children of the negroes. This desire has been considerably strengthened since your leaving England, and I do feel that no earthly tie could keep me from offering to go, did a situation offer, and did it appear to be the path of Providence. I have endeavoured to examine the motives which have induced me to make this choice, and though I have too often discovered them to be unworthy of so noble an undertaking, yet I do trust that they arise from a desire to be useful in the cause of Christ.

"Should it be the will of God that I should go, I think it will be as a schoolmaster. Here I feel in my element, and I should love to engage in it. I do not think that I could be ordained. My talents for public speaking are but small, and if this could not be dispensed with I feel afraid it would prove a hindrance.

"I should not have the least objection to address the natives in Jamaica, but to speak to congregations in England is what I do not think myself capable of. I do still at times go to Thomas Street, and find it pleasant, though I feel a difficulty in speaking without writing first, which I have not time to do; but, perhaps, some part of this might wear off.

"However, preaching does not seem my element; but if a person was wanted to go out as a schoolmaster, and to assist in addressing the negroes at times, it would be the joy of my heart to be permitted to go."

What would the brothers, dear friends as well as brothers, have thought if they could have known what "the opportunity" would be for William's going out?

Thomas, with his heart full of loving service, died after a few days' illness, three months from the time that he landed at Kingston. William, who had longed to go and be *with* him, went to take his place. When the intelligence of his brother's decease was communicated to him by Mr. Fuller, his feelings were strongly excited; but immediately after the first gush of feeling had subsided, he rose from his seat, crying, "Then, if the Society will accept me, I'll go and take his place"

It does not appear that this resolution gave rise to any application to the Society on his part, or that it was even communicated at the time to any of those who conducted its concerns; but Mr. Dyer, the Secretary, had already written to consult Dr. Ryland as to his fitness for the East.

"He is a good printer. I rather question his capacity for learning a language. More suitable for the West Indies." So ran the response. Was Dr. Ryland very naturally looking back, to the days when Carey *would* get some Hebrew out of him or any other minister he met, and to whom no language came unwelcome as a subject of study? And again, "William is a good lad, but not equal to Thomas." "Chiefly distinguished for the exuberance of animal spirits, and the almost irrepressible tendency to frolic, marked rather by incessant activity than by any deep or earnest thoughtfulness," wrote a gentleman at the Borough Road Training School, where he had gone to prepare for his work as a schoolmaster.

But another language was not wanted. As to his vigour, his irrepressible activity, the Master had need of them, and they were freely rendered back in His service.*

On the 5th of November, 1824, he sailed with his bride, Mary Watkins, by the same ship that two years before had taken over his brother Thomas—*The Ocean*, Captain Whittle. A good friend to him was this captain.

The parting from his home at Kettering was full of sadness.

"Since I parted from you," he writes to a friend, "I have had a series of trials to pass through. My beloved mother I have left on a bed of sickness. The feelings of my relations were of the tenderest kind. My dear sister Ann was overcome with grief, and only three of them could endure to say farewell. Nor could my dear mother endure the conflict, though she expressed herself perfectly resigned to the will of God. The artless simplicity of my youngest brother affected me much, and the scene is more easily to be imagined than described."

From this extract it would appear that Mrs. Knibb parted with William, her second large contribution to the welfare of Jamaica, in her chamber and in silent

---

* NOTE.—Twenty years after, a little of this fire showed itself one day at dinner: "Mr. Knibb, how do you stand the climate, sir?" asked a guest in rather a ponderous tone. "*Sit* it when I can't stand it," flashed back across the table.

sadness, or breathing only an expression of resignation to the Divine will. Ill as she was, it would not have been surprising or unnatural if it had been so. It was otherwise, however. After he had left the room she rose from her sick bed, and went to the window, where, with the half undrawn curtain in her hand, she again caught his eye, and in this attitude she addressed to him these memorable words :—" Remember, I would rather hear you have perished in the sea, than that you have disgraced the cause you go to serve." Having said this she sank again on her pillow to suffer and to pray, scarcely less heroic than that devoted son who sped him joyously to his destiny of conflict and of triumph. He landed at Kingston on the 16th February, 1825.

Mr. Knibb speaks from the first in warm terms of interest in the people, and a few lines to his mother disclosed the ballast in his character, which prevented his uncommon vivacity from carrying him into anything regrettable.

"I feel much pleasure," says he, "in looking forward to my engagements, but at times the weight of responsibility almost overwhelms me. I need much of the gracious aid of the Holy Spirit, for I am poor and weak, and without Him I can do nothing. What a mercy it is that He will afford it, and make those who confide in Him instruments of advancing His glory in the earth. Oh, for grace thus to live, that death may be eternal gain!"

Of course, he could not at that date be a day in Jamaica without seeing slaves It is worth notice that his first impression was not of their physical misery, but of the moral evil the system fostered. He writes to his mother:—

"The cursed blast of slavery has, like a pestilence, withered almost every moral bloom. I know not how any person can feel a union with such a monster, such a child of hell. For myself I feel a burning hatred against it, and look upon it as one of the most odious monsters that ever disgraced the earth. The slaves have temporal comforts in profusion; but their morals are sunk below the brute, and the iron hand of oppression daily endeavours to keep them in that ignorance to which it has reduced them. When contemplating the withering scene my heart sickens, and I feel ashamed that I belong to a race that can indulge in such atrocities. It is in the immorality of slavery that the evil chiefly consists. I can easily account for persons becoming familiarised with slavery, and having a dislike to the slaves, as they are very trying; but it ought ever to be remembered that this proceeds from the system, and that the owner has a large portion of the blame attaching to him.

" To proclaim liberty to the captive, and the opening of the prison to them that are bound, is a delightful employment, and here I would dwell that I may be thus employed; with my present views, however, nothing else on earth should tempt me to remain."

CHAPTER II.

FIRST YEARS IN JAMAICA.

WILLIAM KNIBB had been sent out to succeed his brother as a schoolmaster. His first glimpse of the school was taken the morning after his arrival The following account of his reception and impressions he gives to Mr. Fuller :—" The little dears leaped for joy when I entered, and many could not refrain from dancing ; for a negro must express his joy. Many of them are slaves, but the greater part are free. Their writing is excellent, and they improve vastly. Could you visit the school, you would feel abundant cause to say that my brother had not run in vain, neither laboured in vain."

The school improved from the first hour of Knibb's superintendence, and, notwithstanding the climate, he was engaged in it from nine in the morning till three in the afternoon, and had soon the pleasure of seeing order restored within, and of receiving accessions from without. The Admiral then on the station gave him a proof of his confidence, by committing to his care a young African who had just been taken out of a slave-ship. He found that the children made great progress, and felt peculiar pleasure in seeing two slaves—a boy and a girl—at the head of their respective departments in the school.

A new schoolroom was promptly resolved on and built. Its erection was justified by the reception of 150 more scholars in six months. A Sunday-school was also organised, not only for children, but adults ; and, if their teacher loved the merry boys and girls, he was more

deeply touched by watching an aged slave win his difficult way from alphabet to New Testament.

The new schoolroom was followed by a separate apartment for the girls—an occasion for a procession, white frocks and flowers. He could hardly have done the negroes good if he had not entered into their demonstrativeness, the white frocks and nosegays, and dancing for joy.

Engaged in this vigorous teaching, from 9 a.m. to 3 p.m., in the hottest town of Jamaica, Mr. Knibb's health broke down. He was advised to try living at Port Royal, nearer the sea, where he soon became pastor of the church. Port Royal not proving change enough, he undertook the combined stations of Ridgeland and Savanna-la-Mar, hoping that himself and his wife would have better health, by living up at Ridgeland, and only visiting at Savanna-la-Mar, which is on a marshy plain. The following letters refer to his pastoral and private life at this period :—

"To Miss Williams :

"*Sketch of a baptism at Port Royal.*

"Picture to yourself a spacious harbour, about four miles across. Tents are erected at the water-side, and a small portion of the bay is protected by ropes and stakes arranged in a circle. This spot is surrounded by canoes filled with spectators ; the fortifications are covered with people ; all as still as possible. By-and-by you hear distant sounds of voices, and a little band approaches you, two and two, clothed in white, singing as they walk over the sand :

"'Jesus, and shall it ever be,
A mortal man ashamed of Thee ?'

"They arrive ; a hymn is sung, a prayer offered, and, just as the sun sheds its first beams on the Sabbath, we descend into the water ; and there, surrounded by multitudes, I baptize them in the name of the adorable Trinity. When

I was baptizing I was filled with joy and peace, and gave out in the water,

> " ' Why was I made to hear Thy voice,
>   And enter while there's room ? ' "

Death-bed of a Slave.

" I have lately been called to witness the death-beds of some whose experience has rejoiced my heart. One poor female slave, who had been ill of a decline a year, was of the number. I found her lying on a mat on the floor, her head supported by a chest. Never did I see such an object. When I entered, she said, 'Oh, massa, me glad to see you ; me thought me should die, and not be able to tell you how good our Lord is ; Oh, massa, Him too good, too good for me, poor nigger.' After questioning her, I asked her if she was afraid to die ? Her eyes sparkled with delight :—

" ' No, massa, Jesus Him die for me ; me no afraid to die and go to Him—Him too good !' Ah ! thought I, this is religion. Here is a poor slave, with scarcely any comforts, who has been lying for a year in this hut, and can talk of nothing but the goodness of God."

The following, from a letter to his mother, refers to his own feelings :—

" I do enjoy religion here secluded from the world. Though scorned and condemned, I feel that I am the servant of Jesus, and that He will one day vindicate the character of His missionary subjects. *I do enjoy religion.*"

If the black school children were " little dears," how much shall we expect said of twins (William and Mary) of his own ! But the joy soon had its shadow. Little Mary died in ten days and was buried by the side of his (the father's) brother Thomas, leaving the parents clinging with anxiety to the frail life of the boy. He lived, however, to make them very happy.

Take next the chronicle of a seaside holiday :—

"Brooks Pen, Windward Road.

"Well, here I am, wife, child, and all in one of the hottest places under the skies, and yet to me filled with beauty. The owner of this humble place was once a slave, is now free, and is one of the deacons of the church. He invited me here for a day or two; it is about eight miles from Kingston, close to the seaside, healthy and pleasant. The old man sent his horse and chaise for us, and we jogged on farmer like. I think we never looked so family-like before. The chaise was easy and old, the little horse had passed his best days, the harness was none of the best, the black servant was sitting behind, and we three formed one of the oddest appearances.

"In the evening we stood on the seashore, that sea which parts us from England; talked of Bristol friends, sang, 'Jesus shall reign where'er the sun,' and earnestly longed for the time when it should be the case. At ten at night I met a few poor slaves in an old——I know not what to call it : there was a table and a chair and an old lamp under my nose, the smell of which was horrid. Poor things, they had walked far to see me. I sang, 'Come, let us join our cheerful songs' to a negro tune. When I see you I will sing it to you; talked to the poor things about Jesus Christ, read, and prayed with them, and sent them home. They seemed gratified; I was delighted. I meet some more about eleven to-night.

"I wish I could give you an idea of this grotesque establishment; but I am sure I cannot. It is a little, long, square place, with a wooden roof; in our bedroom two hair trunks placed on two stools make a chest of drawers, on which stands the glass. The other room, where the man and his wife sleep, is kitchen, cellar and all. I am now in the hall, where wife is sewing with little Bill in her lap, full dressed in his shirt; around me dogs, pigs, black children, &c. To decorate the walls there is a likeness of their majesties, two looking-glasses, sundry other pictures, and a funnel. Before me rolls the beautiful and wide-spreading ocean, which wafts health to my emaciated frame. After playing awhile with little Will, who holds out his mouth most sweetly to present a kiss, I will try and proceed in my wandering musings.

"I suppose it is natural for folks to talk of their children, and you see I am as foolish as the rest."

From Savanna-la-Mar Mr. Knibb removed to Falmouth in the summer of 1830. Two incidents, connected with the people at Falmouth before Mr. Knibb went to them, are not out of place as showing how eager they were to receive a missionary. They sent frequent deputations, begging Mr. Burchell to write home for a missionary. The narrative is Mr. Burchell's : "The members of one of these deputations having arrived at his house, at the very time he was preparing letters for the packet, they clasped their hands, and dropping on their knees addressed him thus, in the most impassioned tones, 'Write hard, massa ; write hard us, massa.'"

On another occasion, after long and bitter disappointment, one of them, a free man and possessed of a little property, plaintively said, "Come yourself, massa." "I cannot," was the reply. "It shall be no expense to you, massa." "I did not refer to expense, my friend, I cannot preach to my own people with sufficient frequency, but what did you mean by saying it should be no expense?" "I have a house, massa, worth £300 or £400, gained by the savings of my past life, and I will sell it to support the cause." Who can wonder that the missionary continued month after month to "write hard," or at his poignant regret in writing so often in vain.

At last, a Mr. Mann came, dear to many memories, but when he had been settled at Falmouth, he died of fever, after a short but very successful term of labour, and Mr. Knibb, who succeeded him in the spring of 1830, called his new station "the very garden of missionary labour."

CHAPTER III.

"A great door and effectual is opened unto me, and there are many adversaries."

ABOUT the time of Mr. Knibb's arrival in Jamaica there was a lull in the hostility of the planters toward Christianity, especially towards the preaching by dissenting missionaries, and the prayer-meetings of dissenting negroes. It was not in the nature of things that this tranquillity should last long. The people heard the Word gladly, flocked to the meetings, and, what some of the planters liked worse, told one another the good news. Evening meetings were as much as possible stopped, and evening, when the day's work was done, was the one time in the week when the negro could attend; but this passing of the Word from lip to lip, learning a hymn, which, with a negro, means singing it, and praying with one another was very difficult to hinder. The Sunday congregations were crowded. Where it was possible, large meeting-houses were built, and there were many baptisms.

The following instances of negroes who did earnest work among their fellows, and who "endured hardness" as good soldiers of Jesus Christ, are too interesting to pass over.

"Sam" had been a great favourite in his master's house on account of his violin playing. He became a Christian; the prayer-meeting superseded the dance-music with which they were accustomed to make merry.

Fearing lest his musical instrument, which had hitherto been his delight, might now prove a snare to him, he broke it, for he thought that if he sold it he might be tempted to buy another with the money. One day his master told him that he would soon be wanted to play his part as usual.

Without any attempt at concealment, he replied, "The fiddle's broken, master."

"It must be mended, Sam."

"Broken all to pieces, master."

"Well, we must get a new one, Sam."

"I think that no good, master; it will soon be broken."

The master began to suspect this destruction of fiddles must have to do with religion, and, therefore, added in an altered tone, and with a lowering countenance :—

"I hope you do not go to pray, and go after those mad-headed folks, Sam."

"To tell the truth, I have gone, master."

He was now threatened with punishment, and told he should be flogged.

With firmness he replied, "That no good, master, the whip cannot flog the Word out." Dismissed from his easy post in his master's house to toil in a field of labour under a tropical sun, he felt somewhat dejected at first, but soon perceived that an opportunity for doing important good was set before him. In his situation in town he had mingled with a *few* domestics; now he was in the midst of three hundred slaves; he began, therefore, to tell them about his great and gracious Saviour and to invite them to go and hear his minister. Many of them yielded to his invitations and, in a little while, of these three hundred, about one hundred and fifty became regular hearers of the everlasting Gospel. His master heard of this, and felt still more incensed.

Having called for him he addressed him with severity : "How dare you trouble my negroes? I will have no praying negroes."

"Me no tink they be troubled, massa; they do not seem

much troubled, massa. Do they work much worse, or are they much saucy, massa?"

"That is nothing to you. How dare you trouble my negroes?"

"To tell de truth, massa, me think dat the bread dat is good for my soul is good for broder neger, and me think if it be a good thing for me to escape hell it is good for broder neger; and if heaven is a good place for me it is good for broder neger; and me pray, and me pray for my rich massa, and me think if my rich massa would once go and hear the missionary he would always go afterwards."

This was too much for the master's patience; he called the negro "Parson Sam," banged the door, and sent him away. Parson Sam, very thankful to escape so easily, only thought what more he could do for God's glory.

In the evening, when his work was done, he went to some of his master's other plantations to tell his fellow slaves there about the Saviour. He was rewarded by seeing about 500 persons become regular hearers of the Gospel.

Here is the other instance, which attracted more public notice. As it happens, the name again is Sam—but a different man with a different master—and it was not the ill-will of the owner which in this case caused the tyranny.

" Savanna-la-Mar,

"To Mr. Dyer,   "*April* 26, 1830.

"An excellent young man of the name of Sam Swiney, a deacon of my church in this place, is now in prison for his love to Jesus. During my sickness, he and others, both bond and free, met at my house to pray. Information of this was carried to the magistrates, and, though I procured three respectable persons, neighbours, including the head constable, to prove on oath that no noise was made, which the informer had sworn to, the poor fellow was convicted. The magistrate would have it that preaching and praying were the same. I tried to convince him of the difference, but it was of no use ; so for offering a prayer to God, and nothing more, this poor fellow is sentenced to receive twenty lashes on his bare back, and to be worked in chains on the roads for a fortnight. I did all I could to save him, and so did his owner, a respectable gentleman of colour (Mr. Aaron Deleon), who told the magistrates that he had his permission. Next morning I went to see him flogged, determined to support him as well as I could, however painful to my feelings. There he was, a respectable tradesman, though a slave, stretched indecently on the ground, held firmly down by four slaves, two at his hands and two at his feet. The driver was merciful, or every lash would have fetched blood. 'Oh ! what have I done,' was the only exclamation that escaped from his lips, accompanied by a moan extorted by the pain.

" He was raised from the ground, chained to a convict, and immediately sent to work. I walked by his side down the whole bay to the no small annoyance of his persecutors. Amidst them, I took him by the hand, told him to be of good cheer, and said loud enough for them all to hear, ' Sam, whatever you want, send to me and you shall have it.'

"The good people here have behaved nobly to him, encouraging him by every means in their power. I shall see that he wants for nothing, and by my public notice of him show that I consider him a persecuted Christian."

Such was the feeling in the island against Christian negroes. This case attracted much interest in England, and Sam Swiney's liberty was procured for him. The planter-interest did not love the missionaries the better for it, especially when the magistrates who had awarded the punishment were dismissed in consequence by the Governor (Lord Belmore) and the English Minister (Lord Goodrich). This decision arrived in the autumn of 1831 ;—a very critical time.

The spirit of the magistrates may be illustrated by the speech of one* of them to Mr. Burchell :—

"Sir, you missionaries are a body of persons whom we (the legislature) do not acknowledge. You have intruded yourselves on the island unsolicited and unwelcomed. So long as you proceed on your own resources, you are licensed on the principle of toleration; but we have passed this law that you may not raise an income here for carrying on your purposes, and to prevent your further increase among us."

"This law" referred to a clause in the Consolidated Slave Act, forbidding the slaves to subscribe to the expenses of the new chapels or the minister's salary. There were other vexatious restrictions as to hours of meeting and holding meetings among themselves, which were fearfully hard on the slaves, and the penalties meant to enforce obedience were very severe. Three times the Act was sent home to England for the ratification necessary, three times it came back refused by Mr. Huskisson and Sir John Keane, the Lieutenant-Governor. The planters had to give it up and fall back on some old regulations.

Meantime, in the British House of Commons a more aggressive tone had been taken.

On the 15th April, 1831, Mr. Fowell Buxton brought forward a motion relating to British Colonial slavery, and upon this occasion His Majesty's Ministers, although not accepting the terms of Mr. Buxton's motion, announced their fixed determination to take up the subject.

When this became known to the planters of Jamaica, they had recourse to their usual mode of defeating the benevolent intentions of the British Government; they raised a clamour against the measure proposed, and wrought

* Mr. Gregson, Member of the Assembly for the parish.—"*Burchell's Life*," 120.

themselves up to a high pitch of excitement. During the months of July, August, and September, public meetings were held with much excited speaking, and besides these meetings the island was pervaded by a habit of free and passionate conversation among the colonists. Everyone was talking of the proceedings of the British Parliament, everyone said that the King of England was going to give freedom to the slaves, and everyone indulged himself in the unrestrained expression of his anger.

The reader has now before him the whole machinery by which the slave population was thrown into a state of excitement in the autumn of 1831. They had heard that the king was going to set them free, and that their masters were determined to prevent it; but they learnt this through the masters themselves. The parish meetings were open and some slaves were always present; the conversation at table was unguarded. The town slaves got hold of the newspapers, and circulated what they could make out as far as possible. That they should be set free was delightful and exciting to the last degree, that their masters should withhold the boon of the mother country was maddening; and, if possible, the irritation was increased by the violent language in which the planters expressed their rage. The master of one slave told him that freedom was come from England, but that he would shoot every —— black rascal before he should get it. Another heard his master say, " The king is going to give us freedom, but he hoped all his friends would be of his opinion and spill their blood first."

For rough language the Home Government fared no better than the negro slave, only it was too far off to be heard.

A statement made in the House of Commons by Dr. Lushington was called unfounded and treasonable ; another declaration in the same place " bespoke insanity." The allegations of the Anti-slavery Party were stigmatised " as the false and infamous representations of interested and infuriated lunatics." There is a whole page of such amenities.

The Governor, Lord Belmore, did not escape. Appealed to by some of the missionaries, his secretary replied that his lordship had anticipated their petition by a proclamation just promulgated through the island, enjoining the magistrates to find out and punish the authors of such outrages (destruction of chapels, &c.). The proclamation was posted up. Under the copy in the court-house, Montego Bay, was found written :—

"Whoever gives information respecting the above shall entitle himself to be tarred and feathered."

Surely, a threat held over anyone who would obey the Governor was worse treason than anything laid to the charge of the missionaries, who were kept in close custody, while certain magistrates searched their papers in hopes of finding something on which to found an indictment.

One would think that Englishmen, of all people, would sympathise with desires after freedom   They think so much of the liberty of the subject—when *they* are the subjects. Have we to confess that there is another not so generous instinct in them—masterfulness, the craving after someone to rule over, and further that absolute power over their fellow-creatures is an intoxication few can stand, especially when they have satisfied themselves that the fellow-creature is of inferior race, and have possibly shaped their conduct towards keeping him so ?

As Christmas drew near, the irritating elements which the planters had diffused through the slave population began to do their work, under a full, though mistaken conviction, that the king had made them free. It was suggested by a slave named Sam Sharp, that they should not work after Christmas without wages; and in order to engage many persons in concert for this purpose, meetings were held by him on a plantation called Retrieve, from about the middle of October. His plan, and nothing further seems to have been originally intended, was that the drivers when they went at the usual hour for orders on New Year's Day should say, "The people know well that they are free and will not work any more without some satisfaction, we don't rebel, but we work [have worked] long enough for nothing." Some more violent spirits must have entertained a further idea of setting fire to the properties. They thought they had concerted their measures in secrecy, but the planters seem to have known all and were prepared for the outbreak. The slaves had been more successful in keeping all knowledge from the missionaries, their opinions being too well known to admit of any hope of gaining their sanction to it.* Samuel Sharp was executed at Montego Bay, May 30th, attesting with his last breath the innocence of the missionaries, and declaring that, if he had listened to their instructions, he should never have come to that awful end.

But the very fact that their reason for being on the island was the good of the negroes envenomed the planter party, and an evil construction was put upon everything done by them. Thus, it had been agreed many weeks before, that several of the pastors should meet together at Salter's Hill for the sake of special services in connection with opening a new chapel there ; these services were taken to be a blind, screened by which they could meet and conspire, and a good deal of trouble was made in consequence, though at this very meeting Mr. Knibb, as senior missionary present, and spokesman for the rest, spoke so strongly to the slaves as to the falsity of the idea of being set free on New Year's Day, that they accused him violently of being bribed by

---

* Hinton's "Life of Knibb," p. 116.

the planters to deceive them.   He had not long returned to
Falmouth when the news came of an actual outbreak on
the country plantations, and the glow of incendiary fires
could be seen at night.   Then followed some days of
confusion and great apprehension of danger.   The
missionaries were sent for repeatedly to the court-house,
always in great uncertainty how they should be treated.
One day things seemed going well enough, for when told
they must all enlist, Mr. Whitehorne was allowed to make
application for his former rank as captain of militia, and
Mr. Nicholls allowed a pass to go home as he was in ill-
health.

The next day while on guard, they (Messrs. Knibb,
Whitehorne, and Abbott) were arrested.   An hour or two
afterwards they were told that the Colonel had received
such intelligence as had induced him to send them to head-
quarters, for which purpose a conveyance would be ready
in half-an-hour.   Permission to see their wives was refused,
only a memorandum of necessaries and a message to the wives
to go to Montego Bay by land was allowed.   The conveyance
was an open canoe.   It was nearly noon, and they were un-
protected from the meridian sun.   No charge had been
made against them ; the cause of this treatment they knew
not, further than the general clamour of their having
promoted the rebellion ; and this uncertainty of course
augmented their sufferings.   Having spent six hours in
this open canoe they reached Montego Bay, where a great
scene of horror presented itself.   The houses which had
recently adorned the neighbouring hills were now in flames,
and the confusion and noise of war prevailed.   Two men-
of-war were lying near the town, guard boats were flying
about, and on land at a little distance flashes of musketry
were seen announcing that the angel of death was abroad.

On their landing at night, they were first marched to
the court-house, under their armed guard, and then to

MONTEGO BAY.

the lodgings of Sir W. Cotton, where they were kept waiting before the door for half-an-hour, a detention willingly borne, as their wives were able to be with them for a few minutes; thence they were sent to another magistrate, a Mr. Barrett, finally back to the court-house. The missionaries soon discovered that they were considered answerable for the crimes of the slaves, and they were conducted into the presence of Major Coates, the officer of the guard, who told them "that he had received orders from the Custos to put them under guard in that place."

They were placed in the jury-box, which was raised eight or ten feet from the floor. Here they were emphatically "a gazing stock," a candle being placed before them, evidently for the purpose of exposing them to public view. In this situation they had to endure the greatest insults and indignities, and to listen to the grossest language.

On entering the jury-box, Mr. Knibb (who had been ill for a day or two, and whose physical condition was not improved by seven hours' exposure in an open boat, his feet wet all the time) asked permission to lie on the floor, no very great luxury one would say, but the sentry vociferated with awful oaths, "No, you rascal; if you attempt to move an inch, I'll thrust this bayonet through you, you villain;" and at the same time pointed the bayonet to his breast. This man afterwards said, in a conversation with another guard, "This is the notorious Knibb, who robs our negroes of their macaronies; but, never mind, I am happy to say he will be hung to morrow"; he also added, "that he was a ruined man, but he was now compensated for all his losses by the satisfaction he felt at seeing Knibb brought to the gallows." This individual had previously threatened to stab Mr. Knibb for stumbling as he ascended the steps of the jury-box. He said, "it was a shame to put four men to guard these fellows, they ought to be handcuffed and put with the negroes." Mr. Abbott was feeling a severe pain in his back, heightened above its usual degree by fatigue and anxiety. He mentioned this to Mr. White-horne, and wished to shut the window behind him, when this guard pointing his bayonet at Mr. Abbott, said, "Hold your tongue, you rascal; don't speak to that other prisoner again or I'll give you the bayonet, and I won't speak to you twice either, you villain." In the presence of such a man they dared not attempt to refresh themselves with either food or sleep, but rested their heads on a bar which was before them, endeavouring to compose their minds to their situation till the morning.

But, between ten and eleven o'clock a deliverer came named Roby, an old acquaintance of Mr. Whitehorne, and he kindly undertook to use his exertions for the release of all for the night, and after midnight took them to the custom-house.

Next morning he fetched their wives and presented them with a paper * he had procured from Mr. Barrett releasing them on bail, each of them to find a security for £50, and to promise to be ready to appear when called for. It speaks much for the conviction of their innocence that the

---

* Copy of original paper in possession of Rev. D. J. East, late of Kingston, Jamaica.

The Major-General having placed William Knibb, William White-horne and T. Abbott at my disposal, and there being no specific information lodged against them, I have determined that they shall be released on condition that each of them finds a security to the amount of £50; that he will not leave the town of Montego Bay, and will be ready to appear when called on. The security to be entered into before any magistrate.

RICHARD BARRETT, Custos.

Montego Bay, January 4th, 1832.

securities with Mr. Roby were a magistrate * and the collecting constable of Montego Bay.

It is right, after speaking of the spiteful malice of some of
their adversaries, to record with warm gratitude the kindness of other individuals among the class of whites who
were in general opposed to them. Mr. Knibb, in old days at
Port Royal, owed his freedom from annoyance to the
friendship of the senior magistrate of that place. Mr.
Vaughan had stood firmly by Mr. Birchell at Montego
Bay. Mr. Roby candidly told them that though his love of
justice constrained him to interfere, he thought them unin-
tentionally mischievous to the slaves and wished them off
the Island. Where, "love of justice," merged into inde-
fatigable kindness, it is hard to say.

Perhaps our good missionaries Knibb, Abbott, and
Whitehorne were safer on bail than if they had been set
quite free. No service had been attempted on the Sunday
morning,† only family worship at their lodgings, and Mr.
Knibb had read aloud a printed sermon. This grew by
report into preaching to a large concourse of negroes, and
occasioned a summons to the court-house. Some weeks
after their capture they ventured to visit in open daylight a
remarkable cave near them. Of course, it was reported
that there were rebels in the cave with whom they had
an appointment.

Mr. Gardner, who had come into Montego Bay, was
arrested (on the false witness of a negro who afterwards
repented), and added to the number already on bail, and
on the 7th January the *Garland Grove* came to anchor
in the bay, having on board Mr. Knibb's old associate Mr.
Burchell, and a new missionary Mr. Walter Dendy. Mr.
Burchell had returned from a cruise for his health, and
might fairly be considered free from blame as to the

---

* Mr. Maunderson.　　† First Sunday in January, 1832.

disturbances going on, but he was decidedly the negroes' friend and a missionary. So he was immediately put into strict ward on board a man-of-war, in the harbour, and his papers searched for some evidence which might give colour for proceeding against him.

Mr. Dendy, quite new to the field, seems to have been left at large. The printed accounts of these trying weeks select and make summaries of the news. Mr. Dendy kept a diary, which gives a better idea of the reality of the daily horrors among which they lived than any of these printed accounts.

Some of the brethren were on land, others on board ship. They saw one another at intervals, and sometimes under the constraint of supervision ; and every day brought its bad news, for the trouble was not confined to Falmouth and Montego Bay, nor to the Baptist missionaries alone.

Day-by-day the entry begins something like this :— "Report that the Methodist Chapel should be pulled down," brought by Captain Pengelley ; "that they would not let Mr. Burchell alone till they had had his heart's blood," this came through an American friend ; " Mr. Maunderson said," " Mr. Roby came on board with the news," "The lieutenant of the *North Star* came on board with cautionary information," so it goes on.

Reports all of them, and mentioned as such ; but is it not true that the worst of reports is, that one does not know how much to believe or how much to act upon ? Besides, the brethren could hardly disregard the warnings of people who were exerting themselves so much, and undergoing so much inconvenience for their sakes.

Another thing the diary brings to light is, that the conduct of the missionaries won by degrees upon the captain and officers of the *North Star* (the man-of-war lying in the harbour). The captain had unwillingly given some of them refuge for *one* night from the mob. By the morning time he detained them till written security could be had for the missionaries' protection ; and, when a note from Custos Barrett was obtained, still detained Mr. Knibb, against whom the rage seemed strongest.

This quotation is interesting, and does credit to the candour of the officers of the *North Star*, and to the missionaries whose conduct won their good opinion :—

"Mr. Whitehorne informed me that, in conversation with the officers on board the *North Star*, they told him, when first they came into the harbour, they did not think the missionaries implicated ; but, hearing the statements on shore, they supposed the missionaries had something to do with it, and wrote home accordingly. But after they heard the statements of the brethren, they were satisfied with their innocence ; and they now believed the case to be such as they thought it when first they came."[*]

POSTSCRIPT TO CHAPTER III.

The destruction of mission property and of the private property of missionaries was very large and very spiteful. It began with the large and quite new chapel at Salter's Hill, about eight miles from Montego Bay, by a party of the St. James's Militia, under the command of two officers.

To the utter destruction of the chapel at Falmouth a magistrate led the way, employing the St. Ann's Regiment, which had used it as a barracks and was just leaving the

---

[*] Diary, February 9th. The original manuscript of this journal has kindly been put into the hands of the writer by the Rev. D. J. East. Mr. Burchell was so intimately Mr. Knibb's friend and fellow-worker that some extracts from the diary, and from Mr. Burchell's own letters relating to him, are added as an appendix. They throw light, too, on the general state of affairs. Other authorities: *Hinton's Memoir of Knibb*, 79-117 ; *Voice of Jubilee*, 56-60.

town (7th February, 1832).   Montego Bay Chapel followed
next day.   The chapels at Savanna-la-Mar, Brown's. Town,
Lucea, and St. Ann's Bay, were pulled down.   Those at
Fuller's Field, Ocho Rios, and Ebury were burnt.   Others
not destroyed were injured and their furniture wrecked.

There is an ugly list in Cox's History ii. 114, of the
persons known as participators, or using no means to
hinder, including eleven magistrates, fourteen army or
militia officers (those of this standing who were magistrates
are not counted over again), and finishing with the head
constable.   Another list follows of *depredators* of the same
social standing.   Houses belonging to the mission, or the
private property of the missionaries were ransacked, sometimes destroyed.

CHAPTER IV.

DISTURBANCES NOT OVER.

On the 9th of February, 1832, the Custos, Richard Barrett, wrote as under to Mr. Maunderson :—

"MY DEAR SIR,—Having examined the evidence against the missionaries of the Baptist persuasion. in whose behalf you have interested yourself very humanely, I have to inform you that there is no evidence in my possession that implicates Mr. Abbott and Mr. Whitehorne, and no legal evidence implicating Mr. Burchell. These persons must therefore be discharged from their bail.—I am, my dear Sir, your faithful and obedient servant,

(Signed) RICHD. BARRETT, Custos."

The original letter is in the possession of the Rev. D. J. East.

On the tenth of February, as before stated, Messrs. Whitehorne and Abbott were set quite free. Mr. Knibb was still on bail for a few days longer.

On this 10th of February he wrote to his mother: "Whether this will be the last letter you will receive from your son is known only to that kind and indulgent God who has hitherto preserved my unworthy life."

It was the last, not because *he* died, but because *she* entered into peace—a private and tender sorrow for him to bear in the midst of so much harassing annoyance, amounting, from time to time, to very real danger, at his distant post.

The next day, February 11th, he writes, "I looked back on all the goodness and mercy which. the Lord God had caused to pass before me. .This day, seven years ago, I

landed on this island, and do I repent coming? No!
With eternity and a jail in prospect, I do not. I mourn
over my sins, I long to be more active in the service of
God, and earnestly do I pray that I may come forth from
the furnace of affliction purified as gold seven times tried.
Held a prayer-meeting in the afternoon, secretly, for fear of
our enemies, to pray that God would protect dear brother
Burchell, who is fetched as a prisoner on shore.   Heard the
painful news that both he and dear Gardner are recommitted
to jail; may God support them.   O that His glory may be
promoted by us all ! "

"On the 14th Mrs. Knibb went to Falmouth, to look after
the furniture saved from the infuriated whites by our female
friends, and to collect evidence; the Lord in His mercy
protect her ! In the evening heard that I was released from
my bail, having been a prisoner seven weeks, and not any
charge brought against me.   Heard that they were trying to
find one; may the Lord disappoint them, if it be His
will."

"Copy of my discharge, after seven weeks' and one day's
detention

"Montego Bay,

February 14, 1832.

"Having examined the evidence of Samuel Stennett,
Adam, and Paris against —— Knibb, Baptist missionary,
and finding nothing therein to support a criminal prosecution, I declare the said —— Knibb discharged, with his
sureties, from their recognizances,

"RICHARD BARRETT, Custos."

Thus released he went the next day to Falmouth.   The
feeling of the white inhabitants was so violent that his landlord begged him not to return to his house, and he accepted
the entertainment offered by Elizabeth Dunn, a free person
of colour and one of his church members.

Without a home, without even lodgings, for with an angry mob howling round her house, Elizabeth Dunn was frightened into desiring him to leave, with cautions from two gentlemen that there was a plan for murdering him, one of them having been invited to assist in tarring and feathering him, which was to be so managed as to cause death ; with a chapel in ruins and what money he had, lost, his first days of liberty were anything but joyous.

The comfort was to find that his own people, with only three exceptions, had been quite quiet during all the disturbances.* Some of them, in places of trust as foremen or stewards, had saved the estates on which they served. Mr. Knibb gives instances of such in his evidence before the Committee of the House of Commons.†

---

* Perhaps it ought to be made plain that there were two quite distinct sets of mobs—the negroes, who, maddened by the idea that the freedom given by the king was kept from them, rose on the estates; while the men who attacked the missionaries were the roughs of the towns, sometimes connived at, sometimes even led, by a magistrate.

† On Green Park Estate, in Trelawney, where he had thirty or forty members, and eighty or a hundred connected with the church, he stated that they (the negroes) mounted guard every night, and when the rebels came down to set fire to the trash-house, they put it out.

With reference to one man in particular, Charles Campbell, Mr Knibb testifies : " He took charge of the property and defended it. There were twenty-seven Baptists on that property (Weston Favel). The overseer gave everything into the hands of that man ; he was absent about a month, and during that time the man took care of the whole. He turned the people out regularly to work ; and he stated to me that not a single Baptist on the property refused to turn out when the rest did." For his good conduct the man received his freedom from his master.

In this district of the county of Cornwall 74 slaves were rewarded by the authorities. Of these, 25 were Baptists, which, compared with the whole population, makes this proportion—1 slave out of every 500 Baptists; 1 slave out of 1,927 not Baptists.

At any rate after the formal release written by Mr. Barrett, the Custos, Mr. Knibb might believe the charges against him were withdrawn—and that no criminal prosecution would be attempted.   Not so—the planters could not suffer their intended victim so easily to escape.

When the Cornwall assizes met on the 12th of March at Montego Bay, the Attorney-General announced his intention of sending up indictments against Messrs. Gardner and Knibb.   Mr. Knibb heard of it as he was walking along the streets.   He surrendered himself for trial, obtained bail for £1,000 and set to work busily to prepare. Far from being troubled, he was in truth rejoiced at this occurrence, since it would afford him the opportunity he had all along desired of publicly proving his innocence.

The trial of Mr. Gardner actually came on the 23rd, but the case got up against him altogether broke down. Warned by this issue, the Attorney-General at once abandoned the charge against Knibb, by entering a *nolle prosequi*.   This was greatly to Knibb's disappointment. It was however, equivalent to a verdict of acquittal.

It seems a curious contradiction to all that was said against him—that while this trial was pending, on the gravest criminal charge, he was applied to by the Hon. William Miller, Custos, of Trelawney, for assistance, in discovering the place and ramifications of the revolt.   Mr. Miller said he had conferred with the Chief Justice as well as one of the magistrates on the bench, and they agreed they could not do better than ask him to assist them.

After the proceedings at law were abandoned, the malignant spirit of the white population continued to threaten his life.   Mr. Miller and Dr. Gordon sent for him and said : "Mr. Knibb, it is our decided opinion that your life is not safe.   We would do anything to protect you, but we cannot protect you."   By their urgent advice he left that part of the island.

Though thus obliged to leave the neighbourhood of Falmouth for a time, he had no desire to give up his work there. He writes to Mr. Dyer on the 5th of March :—

" I hope I shall not have to leave the island ; 1 feel as if it were impossible to quit the people. Do pray for us. Do entreat the British Christians for us. Many have bound themselves by an oath to murder us. Shall we look and cry to Britain in vain ? I know we shall not to God. Oh, remember our poor slave members ! Their sufferings now would make a heart of stone weep. If something is not done speedily for them many of them will be martyrs. That God in His infinite mercy may guide, bless, keep, and preserve you, and give you and the committee all the wisdom you so much need in this deeply bitter trial, is my earnest prayer."

The destiny which he deprecated, however, awaited him ; his brethren in Jamaica commissioned him to visit England on their behalf, and co-operate there with Mr. Burchell, " on account of his intimate acquaintance with the mission in the disturbed part of the island, and his knowledge of circumstances immediately connected with the rebellion." Mr. Knibb and his family sailed from Kingston on the 26th of April. Just as he was about to leave the island he received credible information that twenty persons had sworn to put him to death. If they had known the work he was to do they would have wanted to kill him three times over !

To the planter-party it was very disappointing. They had not succeeded in procuring the conviction of one of the missionaries for whose banishment they so longed.

Details have been given of one little knot of missionaries, but the same spirit of persecution vented itself on many others in different parts of the island.

There was not only the operation of a severe law strictly carried out ; but there was a spirit of hatred and ruffianism

3*

abroad producing results which, looking back on them through a distance of years, would seem hardly credible if we had not names, dates, and details—these, if untrue, should have been contradicted shortly after their first publication.

For instance, it was said in the hearing of a certain Lieutenant Shenton, that the Governor had borne testimony to the inoffensive and guiltless conduct of the missionaries. Mr. Shenton remarked, "that is but his (Earl Belmore's) opinion, for my part I think it would be best to take out all the missionaries, placing them in a ring with the Governor in their midst, and so shoot them all together."

The intimidation practised on Mr. Knibb's landlord at Falmouth, and upon the good-natured coloured woman who allowed him house-room, has been already mentioned. Any free coloured people who risked an act of kindness to the missionaries were in danger of very rough usage. In proof of this spirit, take the following :—Mrs. Brown, a free-woman of colour residing on her own property, was summoned to appear at Manchioneal, the professed object being to elicit criminating evidence against the missionary, Mr. Burton, who had preached at her place. Her infant was only five days old; and while she lingered at Manchioneal, too weak to return home, Mr. Panton and three other magistrates went to her house to search it. Locks were broken, and barrels of flour and pork rummaged to find the free paper which they supposed Mr. Burton might have left. Miss Duncan, who resided at the house, was struck in the face by Mr. H. W. Speed, a magistrate, during the examination, because she spoke the truth respecting some of his slaves; and Mrs. Brown's mother was struck repeatedly, and knocked to the ground.

Terribly disappointed that the Home Government would

not allow their Consolidated Slave Act, the planter interest devised another scheme. A meeting was called at St. Ann's Bay, on the 26th of January, from which resulted the celebrated compact, entitled "The Colonial Church Union." In furtherance of the object of this meeting, the following paper was placarded at several places on the Bay, and printed in some of the island journals :—

"INHABITANTS OF JAMAICA!

"Your danger is great. If you have discovered the source of your disease, lose not a moment in expelling the poison from your veins. Rally round your church and kirk before it is too late, and defend yourselves from all who attack them : the preservation of your wives, your children, your properties, your houses—nay, of your very lives, demands it. A Colonial Church Union is all you want to unite the friends of the colony in a defence which must then succeed."

This association is said to have caused almost as much annoyance to really religious Church people as to the Dissenters. What was its attitude to the latter, the report of one of its general meetings will show : " Several resolutions were passed, the sixth of which bound the Union to *support* and *protect* the chapel destroyers." This meeting was held on the 15th of February, the day after the mission premises at St. Ann's Bay with the Wesleyan chapel there had been destroyed, and by some of the same party two chapels burnt at Ocho Rios.

CHAPTER V.

" I WILL HAVE SLAVERY DOWN."

"" So long as the islands were peopled by the importation of native Africans, who lived and died in heathenism, the relation of master and slave might be expected to be permanent ; but now that an indigenous race of men has grown up, speaking our own language, and instructed in our own religion, all the more harsh rights of the owner, and the blind submission of the slave, will inevitably, at some period more or less remote, come to an end."

Despatch of Viscount GODERICH *to the* Earl of BELMORE,
Dated the 1st *of March*, 1832.

" What of your own William Knibb ? God raised him up for a special work ; and how wonderful the endowments which He gave him for it ! He was ordained of God to fight the battle of negro freedom. Some preceded him in that holy war. His beloved brother Burchell and others stood side by side with him, and aided in the conflict; but William Knibb led the noble army of emancipation on to the victory.

" Who that knew him will ever forget his holy indignation against oppression and wrong; his manly compassion and tearful sympathy with the down-trodden and afflicted ; his inflexible resolution to snap the fetters of the enslaved, and to bid the oppressed go free ; or that overpowering and impassioned eloquence which, flowing out of the fulness of his heart, bore all before it with resistless force. He was a God-made man, eminently gifted by God Himself for the work which God had given him to do.   " Rev. D. J. EAST,
      ." To the people of Falmouth.

" ' Who knoweth whether thou art come to the kingdom for such a time as this.'—ESTHER iv. 14."

WHEN the pilot came on board the ship in which Mr. Knibb was, in the English Channel, he brought the news that the Reform Bill had passed. "Thank God," exclaimed Mr. Knibb ; "now I will have slavery down. I will never rest day or night till I see it destroyed, root and branch."

He was burdened with anxieties as to how far the Baptist Missionary Society would sustain their missionaries in the great effort of reconstructing the Mission, and how far they would co-operate with him in his active efforts for the overthrow of slavery; these were burdens of thought and heart almost too heavy to be endured.

The policy of the several societies had been to keep as quiet as might be on the subject of slavery, lest a political character should be given to the Mission, and with the feeling that, unless silent, they would be debarred from working among the negroes, and so from giving them the spiritual benefit of which they had been the messengers hitherto, by speaking of God's great grace to their souls. Mr. Knibb, on the other hand, was burning to tell out the truth about slavery; and, in general, about slaveholders. Mr. Price gives this account of Knibb's meeting with the committee :—

"However, we went. Knibb gave a detailed account of his sufferings and those of his brethren, which was received, of course, with the deepest interest. Mr. Dyer exhorted to prudence and a temperate policy.

"At length Knibb stood up, and his words, as near as I can recollect—certainly in substance—were : 'Myself, my wife, and my children are entirely dependent on the Baptist Mission. We have landed without a shilling, and may at once be reduced to penury; but, if it be necessary, I will take them by the hand and walk barefoot through the kingdom ; I *will* make known to the Christians of England what their brethren in Jamaica are suffering !' I [Rev. Thomas Price] believe I was the first to speak after this declaration; and, I need not say, I exhorted him to stand by his avowal, and assured him of the sympathy and co-operation of many."

At the annual meeting of the Society on the 21st of June, Messrs. Phillippo and Knibb were to represent Jamaica. The former spoke tenderly and interestingly on the way the blacks had welcomed the Gospel. Mr. Knibb followed on *Slavery*. He had been warned to be moderate, but he declared that he could no longer restrain himself. The warning touch was presently given. It was a solemn moment, and the man was made for it.* He paused, gave a lightning glance at the awful atrocities of the past, the glorious possibilities of the future, and the grandeur of his own position, as encompassed with terrible responsibilities; then, concentrating all the energies of thought, feeling, and voice, he exclaimed: " Whatever may be the consequence, I will speak. At the risk of my connection with the Society and all I hold dear, I will avow this ; and if the friends of missions will not hear me, I will turn and tell it to my God ; nor will I desist till this greatest of curses—slavery—is removed, and, 'Glory to God in the highest,' is inscribed on the British flag ! "

The hesitation was over. The thrill passed through the assembly, through the Christian Church, through the country. There was to be no more silence as to the state of things in the colonies, that by silence the missionary might be tolerated in preaching to the slaves. The slave was to be free !

---

* Authorities have been given and care has been taken not to colour them   Here is a piece of oral tradition.   A gentleman present at this meeting, or one held soon after, told the mother of the writer that he found himself next to a returned Jamaica missionary of another denomination.   As Knibb's narrative poured from his lips, he heard his neighbour's undertoned comment; "How dare he ! How dare he ! He can never go back ! " " Do you mean that it is not true ? " asked our informant.   " True ; yes, every word of it ; but how foolish, foolish, he can never go back ! "   But the power of the testimony worked on the listener, and, presently when his turn came, he confirmed every word that Knibb had uttered.

Mr. Dyer writes : " It must be evident to the dullest capacity, and is universally seen and felt here, both by friend and foe, that either Christianity or slavery must fall. Unless slavery be extinguished, the hope of freely publishing the Gospel in Jamaica is fallacious. Instead, therefore, of picking leaves off the tree, we are laying the axe at the root with all the strength we can command, and, by God's blessing, will not cease to do so till its fall be accomplished."

At other meetings in London, and everywhere over England, Knibb went to bear his testimony. The story wanted no working up; just the same over again at different places : the power that slavery gave to a master to oppress his slave, and the effect this power had on the master to make him a tyrant. There were noble men, as we have seen, in this narrative, and to whom Mr. Knibb bore witness, on whom the smell of the fire had not passed; but what of the naturally tyrannical, the naturally irascible? What of the weak, who could not withstand temptation? And what of the victims of such men and women? And if idle, dishonest negroes got no more than their deserts, it was into the souls of those who desired to live an honest, sober, and godly life that the iron entered; those who had picked up a little education, and had, in spite of every obstacle, grown into something like manliness, felt their bonds the heaviest. Of course, the religious among them felt it most of all. And when such fell into the hands of men who hated the Gospel, they were made to suffer terribly. At a distance of time, speeches read tamely; spoken, and at the time, these statements set forth by a warm-hearted man, who thoroughly believed what he said, were instinct with life and fire.

Sympathy was evoked all over the country. Not only warm-hearted feeling, but principle had been awakened

from a long sleep, and with open eyes saw right from
wrong. Now came the contest for lawful authority to
do the right. It began as all such battles should begin,
with a day set apart for united and importunate suppli-
cation to Almighty God. This was on April 20th.
Christian missions were not alone in the fight; they
could hardly be said to be the first in the field. For
many years the Anti-Slavery Society had been at work,
led by Clarkson and Sturge, while Wilberforce and Buxton
had their party in the House of Commons, a minority
certainly, but an influential minority which had been
instant in season and out of season in their efforts to
induce the Government and people of England to do
justice to the oppressed children of Africa. They had
as supporters a host of devoted men of all sections of
the Christian Church.

Their first object had been the abolition of the slave-
trade; but now the set time for releasing the slaves
already in the colonies had come. A reformed Parliament
was returned, the members of which for the most part
were pledged to emancipation. The Christian Church
was aroused to action by the events which had occurred
in Jamaica, and by the burning eloquence of Knibb and
other missionaries, who had been witnesses of the negroes'
sufferings. The people at large were appealed to by their
sense of justice, and their love of liberty; and the tide of
public feeling in favour of emancipation rolled on daily,
acquiring new strength, till it became like a resistless torrent,
and petitions from all parts of the country, and from all
classes of men, were poured into the Houses of Lords and
Commons, praying with an importunity that would take
no denial, for the total and immediate abolition of
slavery.

In the middle of May, 1833, Mr. Stanley, afterwards
Earl of Derby, Secretary of State for the Colonies,

introduced into the House of Commons " An Act for the Abolition of Slavery throughout the British Colonies, for Promoting the Industry of the Emancipated Slaves, and for Compensating the Persons hitherto entitled to their Services." Of course, the Bill pleased nobody. It was not enough for the anti-slavery party; it was too much for the planters. Mr. Knibb was called from his public meetings to give evidence before the Committees of the Houses of Lords and Commons; to say again just the same facts he had so often pleaded; this time in cool, business fashion, and on oath. Wherever he was, it was the same story; as true on the platform as when answering questions in Committee; as full of heart before the Committees as in the public meeting. It burnt so into the heart of good Lord Harewood that, after a sleepless night, he called Mr. Knibb into a private room to inquire into the management of his own estates. Mr. Knibb was glad to be able to tell him that the manager—a moral man himself—did what he could for the good conduct of those under him. " I should have slept had I known that last night*; promise me if you find anything of the kind going on on my estate you will immediately inform me." The expression of perfect confidence and the hearty shake of the hand with which the interview concluded, formed a refreshing episode in the six days' strict cross-examination, from the 13th to the 20th July.

The friends of the slave worked hard to free the Abolition Bill from what they considered its objectionable features. They succeeded in inducing the Government to shorten the apprenticeship to six years, and to insert a clause in the Bill to secure to the apprenticed negroes the full use of the Christian Sabbath, and liberty to attend any place of worship they chose,

---

* Of course, this refers to evidence given the day before.

without any denial or interruption whatever. To meet the requirements of the slave-owners, and to secure their co-operation in carrying out the abolition, the Government changed the loan of £15,000,000 into a grant of £20,000,000.

William Knibb had gone out young, as a schoolmaster. From sheer want of enough men who were in any way suitable, he became the pastor of a church and a preacher, without academical instruction or training. At first, on his return to England, his manner was not graceful, says Mr. Eustace Carey, his fellow deputation, nor was his diction rich, nor were his words tastefully selected. His topics were limited in number, his illustrations were constantly repeated, and he was speaking to assemblies who carped at every sentence. Yet, continues Mr. Carey, "I have witnessed congregated masses in that city (Edinburgh) burning and almost raving with indignation at the slave system, as he depicted its cruelties and demonstrated its crimes. His tact and self-possession in a little time became so remarkable that he would easily convert adverse and startling occurrences into an occasion of profit, and even of triumph to his cause." Mr. Carey instances the second meeting held in Edinburgh. "A dense crowd had assembled, but Mr. Knibb was depressed, embarrassed, and showed it plainly at the beginning of his speech, which seemed likely to become a failure. As in this condition he narrated some of the hardships of the slaves, a stentorian voice shouted from the other end of the place, "That is a lie."

The stranger was called up to the platform, where, as far as chairman and deputation were concerned, he had his say out, but not without note and comment as it went along, from the audience. He did Mr. Knibb service; all the depression and embarrassment were gone. The pro-slavery advocate had quoted "Servants, obey in all things your masters according to the flesh." "It is a pity," said Mr. Knibb, as he rose to reply, "the gentleman did not read a little further ; he would have found written ' Masters, give unto your servants that which is just and equal, knowing that ye also have a Master in heaven.' "

The meeting resolved itself into one of the most interesting and influential he ever held in Scotland, and the effect of it followed to the end of that important itinerary.

"His topics were limited." But what topics ? Single-hearted and quite sure of his facts ; speaking not for his own reputation but that the slaves might go free, he had all the charm of a man who was heartwhole on one idea, and that an unselfish one. But all in-born qualifications as brought out by circumstances failed to account for his marvellous power over multitudes. Must we not say that it " was given him in that hour what he should speak " ?

Here is another instance in which Bunyan's story comes true of the fire on which a man continually threw water but which burnt brighter and brighter because it was as constantly, but secretly, supplied with oil. The words are Mr. Saffrey's, who was travelling with him, and being taken ill in the night sought his assistance. "It was about three in the morning, and I was surprised, on entering his chamber, to see him on his knees. On expressing my regret for having intruded on him at such a time, he said, "Never mind. I was anxious to secure some time for prayer this morning. Without doing so I should be afraid to trust myself to reply to the attack of that newspaper." (The newspaper attack had been malignant.)

The incessant moving about did not eclipse his regard for private friends. Here is an instance to Mr. Abbott, dated Beverley, September, 1832, in which he sends warm messages of thanks to Messrs. Maunderson and Lewin, and to his own people : " Have the kindness to send to my dear flock at home. My heart yearns over them. Tell them to

draw together, to pray much, to love each other much, and
in their different stations to act as in the fear of God. Oh,
how I long to be among them! The state of the churches
here makes me love Jamaica more than ever. I will try and
write to them soon, but shall trust to you to comfort their
hearts." *

To his brother Edward he wrote from Norwich his delight
"in finding his sister-in-law a disciple of the lowly Jesus,"
and goes on to ask whether his brother had made a public
profession of Christianity. "Have you yet devoted yourself
to the service of the Redeemer? If you feel the love of
Christ . . . and the necessity of the Holy Spirit to
guide, to cheer, and to counsel you, then go to the people
of God and say, 'This people shall be my people, and their
God shall be my God.'

His letters to his wife are simple private letters. In all
the press of constant moving, so tired sometimes "that he
did not know what to do with himself," they show that he
was going on from day to day in great anxiety as to his
eldest boy William. He writes to his wife begging for news,
giving the most probable addresses, one of which will find
him, always with the patient "if you can" following the
direction where to write, as only those say it, who consider
how difficult it is for a mother nursing a sick child, to turn
to correspondence.

The very charm of these letters is that they are common-
place. He has been to Edinburgh; St. Andrews; Dundee,
with a few words about each; so and so has been very
kind; the weather has been cold; and so forth; but all
intensely affectionate, going into details of his wife's comfort
and very anxious about his boy. Yet there is a good deal
in a little sometimes. Some one had given him *for himself*
a present of £5. He is going to get out of it : a greatcoat ;
a picture frame ; and a present for his wife ; and in strange

---

* See letter, p. 63.

juxtaposition, the next sentence runs, will she write to so and so and enquire the possibility of buying Mary, the wife of Lewis Williams, will she enquire the price, and he will procure the money. Then from the redemption of the slave Mary Williams he turns to his sick boy. A letter has come in. "Your welcome letter reached me ; I had been exceedingly anxious respecting dear William, and return thanks to that kind Father who has so mercifully preserved him." This is from Newcastle, when returning from the Edinburgh meeting ; of the excitement, of the success there, not a word.

From Cork a little gleam of fun shooting across his intensity shows itself for a moment. " Expecting that I shall find a letter from you on my return to Dublin, I seize the earliest opportunity of *answering* it. This you will say is in true Irish style." He carried the sheet back with him to Dublin, where it became a true answer, for he was not disappointed of his letter. Once he touches a tender subject, the salvation of children, old enough to do wrong, and know they are doing it, and manifesting no beginnings of faith, but still *children* : "a mysterious subject, fitter to be prayed over than speculated on."

There is one more episode completely in private life. A little son had been born to him, October, 1832, and named Andrew Fuller. The father's heart was divided between joy at this new gift, and anxiety for his first born. William recovered, but the fifteen months old baby lies buried beside his great namesake at Kettering.

On the 28th August, 1833, the magna charta of negro liberty having passed the House of Lords and Commons, received the Royal Assent, and became law.

The following is its most important clause : " Be it enacted that all and every person who, on the first day of August, one thousand eight hundred and thirty-four, shall be holden in slavery within any such British Colony as aforesaid shall upon, from, and after the said day, the first of August, 1834, become to all intents and purposes free, and discharged from all manner of slavery, and shall be absolutely and for ever manumitted, and that the children hereafter born to any such persons, and the offspring of such persons' children shall in like manner be free from their birth, and that from and after the first day of August, one thousand eight hundred and thirty-four, slavery shall, and is hereby utterly and for ever abolished, and declared to be so throughout the British colonies, plantations, and possessions abroad."

Thus, after years of toil and self-sacrifice, God answered the prayers of His people on behalf of their oppressed fellow-men.

His testimony borne, Mr. Knibb's idea was to go speedily back to his people, but another important thing remained, and he and Mr. Burchell set themselves to that object. The chapels had been purposely destroyed, often the ministers' houses. The island authorities declined altogether to give any compensation, though in many cases they had encouraged the destruction when a firm interference would have saved the property.

They were receiving £20,000,000 for the terrible loss of having to pay their workmen instead of employing slave labour. The chapels were burned, so much the better for their side of the question.

There was nothing to do but (helped by Mr. Buxton's powerful influence) to appeal to the Imperial Government at home, which allowed first, £5,510, the amount of unpaid debt on the demolished properties, and secondly, on further application, £6,195, being one half of the remaining loss sustained, £12,390, on condition that the other half was undertaken by the society.

The sympathy roused was very warm. On the 7th of

August, twenty-one days before passing the Emancipation
Act, a public meeting was held at the London Tavern
to receive the offerings of the churches to restore the
ruined chapels, and bid farewell to the two noble men who
by their zeal and eloquence had so largely created the
deep interest on behalf of the slaves. The amount asked
for was the £6,000, but upwards of £10,000 was brought
in, increased during a few days more to £13,000.

This attained, Mr. Knibb and his family left London
for Jamaica on the 27th of August, 1834, Mr. Burchell
leaving two days after and returning *via* the United States.

Of course, neither of them were in Jamaica on the day
of emancipation. The following remarks on the observ-
ance of this day in Jamaica are from Mr. Burchell's
memoirs. "This peaceful joy, this delicacy towards the
feelings of others, was all that was to be seen, heard or
felt on that occasion, over all the chain of the Antilles.
Amusements there were none, not even those by which
they occasionally beguiled the hard lot of bondage, they
kept as a sacred Sabbath the day of their liberation.
From an early hour their sanctuaries were the central
points of attraction ; young and old alike pressing forward,
not coldly to comply with a formal ceremonial, not to
give mouth-worship or eye-worship, but to pour the full
and warm tides of their hearts in praise to the Giver
of all good."

Mr. Phillippo, who had returned to the island, speaks in
the same terms of the morning services of the day of
emancipation. He quotes the prayer of a negro which
so embraces the subject of the day that it may be
given here. "Since Thou hast done this great thing,
oh, that we may love Thee and Thy Gospel more ; may
we be diligent in our proper calling, fervent, serving the
Lord ! O Lord ! now do Thou make Thine arm bare,

and turn the hearts of all the people to Thee. We bless
Thee that Thou hast inclined so many poor dying sinners
to come up to Thy house this day. O Lord ! teach their
hearts, turn them from their own ways, the same as Thou
didst the city of Nineveh."

The service over, there was a distribution of many little
presents which had been entrusted to Mrs. Phillippo while
in England as keepsakes of the day ; and then it was the
school children's turn to be made as happy as possible.
Accounts of the same kind arrived from all the stations.

Surely the influence of the Christian negroes shows their
religion to have been strong and consistent. The accounts
of large meetings held, of very exciting days, and crowds
collected without riot or drunkenness ; of the quiet, orderly
Sundays that set in with the apprenticeship, make one
think that the Christians were in the majority. It was not
so. The Baptist Church at Falmouth, for instance, with its
regular attendants, who were waiting for membership till
the times were settled and they got their minister back,
might be reckoned at 2,000. There were other congregations in the same place—Presbyterian, Wesleyan, Congrega-
tionalist, beside the English Church, of which no statistics
are at hand. If we reckon these at 5,000, still the 18,000
to 20,000 blacks of the parish who were not in attendance
at any Sunday services outnumber the churchgoers as three
to one, and among this majority were the incendiaries who
had fired the estates. A riotous *minority* will often lead a
number exceeding their own ; yet on Emancipation Day
and other great holidays of that time all was orderly and
quiet. It is always easier for noise and excitement to lead
than for the quiet party ; yet this time the prayer-meeting
led. Hollow Christianity would not have done it, nor
sincere, but weak, sentimentality ; there must have been
truth and strength, and God's guiding spirit among the
people.

CHAPTER VI.

VARIOUS cases of persecution had occurred during the time Messrs. Knibb and Burchell had been in England. Messrs. Dendy, Abbot, Nichols, and others had been in prison, and in many districts no services were allowed.

Mr. Knibb's large church had been left as sheep without a shepherd. He was working for them with all his heart, but was not allowed to work with them. The 885* members in communion, besides regular attendants and children, had no minister to speak to them. Their chapel had been destroyed, the ministry was forbidden. They met together as they could, in little groups "for conversation."

It was not till February, 1833, that Mr. Nichols visiting the place got permission with some difficulty to preach to the *free* people, the first service after the disturbances. The congregation increased in spite of all disadvantages. The first place of meeting held barely 200 people for an audience of 500. A shed was run up, from which they had presently to take one side and attach a large awning to shield the hearers from the tropical sun. To this shed belongs the historical interest of having sheltered as far as it could the large congregations of the day of emancipation, August 1st, 1834—the day when they exchanged slavery for apprenticeship. Six large spaces had been cut out of

---

* This refers to Falmouth ; the outlying stations increased the number by 100, and more than doubled the candidates for baptism awaiting his return.

the walls that persons on all sides might share the proceedings within it. The people collected on this day nearly £60 towards the re-erection of their chapel. The congregation was reckoned at not less than 1,600 persons, and the day passed off in a perfectly orderly manner. There was joy, but no riot, nor even noise—a fact with great justice ascribed to the influence of the Gospel and that of the persecuted men who had preached it.

Mr. Dendy took this opportunity of making known to the people the resolution of the British and Foreign Bible Society to present a copy of the New Testament, with the Psalms, to those apprentices who either could read or whose children were learning to read; and those who could claim the gift came forward with eagerness to have their names entered for the purpose.

Mr. Knibb's return, October 25th, 1834, was too late for his presence on this emancipation day. His arrival, however, had a joy and excitement of its own. He describes his landing at Rio Bueno:

"The people saw me as I stood on the deck of the boat. As I neared the shore I waved my hand, when they, being fully assured that it was their minister, ran from every part of the bay to the wharf. Some pushed off in a canoe, into which I got, with my family, and soon landed on the beach. We were nearly pushed into the sea by kindness. Poor Mrs. K. was quite overcome. They took me up in their arms, they sang, they laughed, they wept, and I wept, too. 'Him come; him come, for true.' 'Who do come for we king, king Knibb. Him fight de battle; him win de crown.' On they rushed to the chapel, where we knelt together at the throne of mercy.

"On the following morning we started by land for Falmouth. As I entered I could scarcely contain my feelings; nor can I now. The news spread, and from twenty to twenty-five miles distant the people came, 'Now

Massa we see enough, him dead; him live again. God bless you Massa for all the good you do for me.' ' God him too good.'

" In the evening we had a prayer-meeting.

" On the Sabbath-day when the people could come from the country, the scene was the most interesting I ever beheld. In the afternoon we celebrated the Lord's Supper. After the service two African women came to me each with her infant born after the 1st of August. When they presented their children and thanked me for their freedom, my feelings completely overcame me I left them, and retired to weep."

" Nothing can be written with greater simplicity than this narrative, and nothing can be more fitting than that the circumstances it details should be placed on record." So writes Mr. Hinton, adding that Mr. Knibb requests as he closes, that if his letter is printed, whatever savours of egotism may be expunged.

The first object naturally was to rebuild the chapel. The shed and awning contrivance was temporarily replaced by a large tent given by W. B. Gurney, Esq.,* and when obliged

---

* A note written by Mr. Knibb to Mr. Gurney's daughters may not be without interest :—

" FALMOUTH,
"*April 20th,* 1835.

" MY DEAR FRIENDS,—

" I take the liberty of sending each of you a ruler made by one of my deacons from a portion of one of the pillars of my old chapel in this town that was destroyed in the riots of 1832.

" I thought that you would perhaps feel some interest in possessing a small portion of the wreck of our mission property, and have therefore sent it.

" The church here is prospering; the number that attend is really astonishing. Last Sabbath I think I had full 3,000 hearers, though the chapel will not hold more than 600.

" The tents are very useful indeed. I know not what I should do without them. Underneath them our Sabbath-schools are held and

to take that down, leave was actually obtained to use the very Court-house where the declaration was signed that Mr. Knibb should never preach any more, and which had since been put to happier use by Lord Mulgrave, when he had the slaves collected there to tell them that they were to be free.

The building time was harassing beyond that of most chapel building, for the contractors failed, but the people generously conquered their difficulty, and the debt was liquidated on the first anniversary of the opening. "We will have it off," said the people. "Let us know if what we bring is enough, if not we will try again." "They gave their all," writes Mr Knibb; "I believe many who gave had not fourpence left."

Of the money collected in England Mr. Knibb had a grant of £3,000. The chapel to be large enough for the people was to cost £6,000, and this outlay was increased by the failure of the contractors.

Another absorbing interest was the admission of new members to the church. After the recommencement of services, Mr. Nichols and Mr. Dendy had looked after Mr. Knibb's stations as well as their other duties would allow, but it had not been thought desirable to add to the church roll. The number of inquirers had risen to about 1,000.

---

numbers listen to the sounds of mercy. Yesterday morning I had the pleasure of baptizing ninety-two in the sea. Their simple confessions of the change wrought in their hearts delighted me. Full 3,000 spectators were present, and the utmost decorum prevailed

"To-day I am fatigued, having preached twice yesterday, administered the Lord's Supper to full 900 of my members, besides the baptizing, &c , &c.

"Among the individuals baptized was a young man who had been a preacher among the Wesleyans for several years. He was once a soldier in the regiment in which Chamberlain, our missionary in the East, was made so useful, and is the only one left alive that was in India at that time."

They were not for the most part new Christians, most of them having been regular attendants before the disturbances began. Of these, 138 were selected for the first baptisms, about three months after Mr. Knibb's arrival in the Island. Many of these spoke of the blessing that Mr. Mann's short but fervent ministry had been to them. His harvest was ripe now. Other baptisms followed as more and more of the eager applicants could be seen, and wise inquiries made about them.

It may be as well to quote here the method used with these and other candidates. Mr. Knibb writes : "Either myself, Mrs. Knibb, or some one whom we know to be fully competent, speaks individually to the candidates, Mrs. Knibb generally taking the females. To each man I speak myself, and hear his views of divine truth. When Mrs. Knibb has spoken to the females, on receiving her report, I talk with them, either individually or collectively. I do not think I ever fail speaking to them in some such manner as this : " You have assured me that you love Christ—that you pray to Him every day—and love to do so—that you are not living in any known sin. You do not believe that baptism will save you, nor the Lord's Supper—nothing but the blood of Christ ? You voluntarily profess to love Christ; no one forces you ; if you do love Him, He will bless you; if not, I beseech you not to put on His name."

He further describes how he calls over the names of those already seen and examined, at a church-meeting, charging those present, if they know anything against any of these candidates to come to him and tell it ; giving a week for this purpose.

Once in the year the church deputed some of the deacons or other active members to visit every property where there were members ; and the investigations were minute and important, as the reports demonstrate. They are all concluded with the statement, "Love prevails."

Then came the question of education. In each of the large districts allotted to our missionaries several schools were necessary to keep pace with 'the demand of the time. When home in 1832, Mr. Knibb had estimated the number of his congregation who could read at about fifty; in February, 1836, he counts them, including children, at 600. This had been brought about by the gratuitous kindness of some of his people on the different estates in setting up evening schools. Falmouth, he said, could take care of itself if the outlying estates were left to their fate. It was the village stations and schools, with urgent need for some sort of room to be used for meetings, as well as schools, which loaded him and his people with expense, and yet, with "from 18,000 to 20,000 apprentices in this parish alone," receiving no instruction and attending no place of worship, how were they to give up all effort for them? The correspondence of this date has constant reference to these stations, six, eight, or ten miles from Falmouth. One quotation is just as apt as another—this one is about Silver Grove. It might, with difference of detail, be Refuge, Waldensia, or Wilberforce, or Suffield

"I enclose," says he, "a plan of a plot of land which is to be conveyed to the Society on Silver Grove, where Camberwell School is now held. It is a most important station, and, as the proprietor has, through his attorney, George Gordon, Esq., promised to give it, I have earnestly to request that you will have a title prepared as soon as possible, conveying it in trust to the Society, and let it be presented for signature in the most acceptable manner as speedily as possible. We have in the neighbourhood full 1,000 persons connected with us; there are 140 in the day, and 250 in the Sabbath-school, and this is the only spot of land that can be procured."

How to supply teachers? There were no, or next to no, teachers with any training at all, nor a coloured

Christian minister with any fit education even for a village charge. For Falmouth School he speaks of getting out a well-trained man from the Lancastrian Schools; for Wilberforce he had "a very pious and intelligent young man in training with Mr. Burchell's schoolmaster at Montego Bay," to act as day schoolmaster, Sunday-school superintendent, and holding of the Sunday service (reading one of Burder's village sermons), if no other supply was within reach. "I have three such schoolmasters, I have also twenty active Sabbath-school teachers who are doing all they can; thus three Sabbath-schools, three day schools, and three evening schools are in constant operation; while three chapels in a dense population of full 16,000 persons are constantly open. The only way in which it is possible to train these young teachers is in schools; they are married, and must be supported.

"Constant preaching, the supply of the stations and schools,. the redressing the injuries of the poor people, and the general interests of the mission, engross all my time. That men will arise here I have no doubt, and I shall hail the day; but education must precede it."

At Endeavour, one of the deacons had begun a school and held a Sunday service. The people there had put up a shed. It was eleven miles from Falmouth; separate service and school were excusable at the distance.

Government grants in aid were accepted for Wilberforce and Suffield, in the difficulty of much money being wanted and other resources very much strained.

Very busy work it was, not only at Falmouth and its outlying stations, but wherever a devoted missionary had his centre station in a town, with knots of people in the plantations for miles round. But evangelisation and church organisation, incessant as their claims were, could not be allowed to engross all the attention; it became more and more apparent that the apprenticeship system was not working well Some things the negroes must have gained, but on the whole the treatment of the apprentices was still such as to slaves. New treadmills were erected, stories of exceptional cruelty varied the monotony of every-day injustice. The apprenticeship law passed by the House of Assembly in Jamaica was "very bad," "I pray God that it may be disallowed." The slaves—those who had saved some money—had been eager to buy up their time, as allowed by England, and go quite free. Prohibitory prices were put on them. "The fact is," Mr. Knibb writes, "that under the Abolition Act they were purchasing themselves so fast that the Jamaica law was made to stop them."

On the 24th of February, 1835, he writes . "Some of the special magistrates flog most cruelly, and I fear will create much discontent. If the Anti-Slavery Society were to send out one or more staunch men, who would be present at the trials of apprentices, and faithfully report them, they would do great good. It would be a check upon the magistrates which they would much feel." In fact the well-known and honoured friends of the slaves, Joseph Sturge and Thomas Harvey, arrived soon after. They came to the West Indies for the express purpose of ascertaining, by personal observation and inquiry, whether the Act of Emancipation was being honestly carried out. They visited the mission stations, where they had opportunities of hearing from the lips of the people themselves, accounts of the sufferings they endured.

On the 1st of June Mr. Knibb writes again : " Oh, this thrice-accursed apprenticeship ! Nothing but blood, murderous cells, and chains ! I think nearly forty young and old females pass my door in chains every morning. Not one school is yet established, while most abominable cells and treadmills are being erected all over the island ! This is to prepare the poor things for freedom !! You tell me to be quiet, and I am ; but if I were at home, I would publish what I know as far as I could travel."

But when it came to not only putting women on the treadmills, but flogging them while upon it by two men at once, Mr. Knibb sent affidavits of two such cases to the Governor himself, and got redress for certain grievances. But the thing remained as a whole, relieved only by the personal character of those managers who were not tyrannical. The feeling grew stronger and stronger that the term of apprenticeship ought to be shortened. The friends of the negro worked for that in England. The Marquis of Sligo,* who had large estates on the island, set all his people free without waiting for legislation, and so did some others. There grew up a strong conviction that the *Christian* people on the island ought to give up their apprentice slaves, and the missionaries did their best to persuade their flocks. Mr. Knibb had some such in his own congregation, most of them people who had little else in the way of property, of whom he writes :—

"To Mr. STURGE.

"FALMOUTH,

"*July 11th*, 1837.

" I have to convey the pleasing intelligence that the poor members of my church who hold apprentices have resolved, one and all, to set them free on the 1st of August, and that the manumissions of most are already in my possession.

---

* The governorship of the Marquis of Sligo, although of brief duration, embraced a most difficult period of the island's history. Society was in a transition state : the masters having to learn the duties of consideration and equity in reference to their inferiors, and the peasantry to acquire the sentiments and habits of free men. Towards each class his lordship maintained an honourable bearing. The paternal character of his administration had so won on the negroes, that they raised a subscription among themselves, in order to purchase a piece of plate for presentation to him.

I requested each of them to make it a matter of prayer,
and when the result came I wept for joy. Not one has
held back. When the first came and signed, 'There,' she
said, 'I have now an easy conscience.' Another said, 'I
have long wished to do it, but I have two children to
support, and they are my all; but I can now trust God.
My heart is at rest.' Others blamed me for not telling
them of it before; and all have said that they have given
the apprentices up from a firm belief that it was sinful to
retain them. I have been to several persons in the town,
and have succeeded in obtaining the manumissions of
eight or ten more, and I am trying to interest others in the
matter. On the 1st of August I shall publicly read the
manumissions in the chapel, and shall address the freed
people and the apprentices that are left, who do not belong
to Christian owners. I shall have a high day, and, blessed
be God, the last vestige of slavery will be removed from
the members of the church."

The writer can well remember hearing her mother say of
the day of emancipation, "If I had been in Jamaica I
should have lived through the day and died *for joy* at
night." She little thought how nearly this was literally true
of another, and that other Mr. Knibb's eldest son, the boy
William, whose health had caused him so much anxiety
while in England. He entered into his parents' warm feelings for abolition, and his mother herself told years after how
fond the negroes were of him, and how proud when "little
massa" could undertake to play for the Sunday services in
chapel. The day when he heard that the members at
Falmouth would agree to set their apprentices free, he
spent in eager joy, but at night fever took possession of him,
and in a few hours it became certain that the day which
had begun with his parents in such joyous thankfulness
must be reckoned as the beginning of a terrible sorrow.
He died on the 25th of July, and the bereaved father went

from the loss of his "brightest earthly hope" to distribute the formal free certificates to such apprentices as had belonged to his own people. Alas! for the high day anticipated. How heavily some of the Lord's people to whom He gives great success seemed ballasted. Little Andrew Fuller died in the midst of his father's successful public meetings in England, and was left to sleep by the side of his great namesake, and now William, the first-born, and developing so much as his father could wish, is taken away.

In another year, August the 1st, 1838, complete freedom was granted, two years before it had been originally intended that the apprenticeship should cease.

Throughout the whole of the British West Indies this 1st of August was a day of unparalleled and unbounded rejoicing. Nowhere was it more joyous than in the island of Jamaica, and nowhere in Jamaica were the demonstrations of gladness more energetic or more characteristic than in Falmouth, where alone it is the writer's business to describe them, and even there, only so far as Mr. Knibb was concerned in them.

On the evening of the 31st of July the Baptist chapel was opened for worship, a transparency, with the word FREEDOM, having been placed over the front entrance to the chapel-yard. A crowded congregation filled the place an hour before midnight and continued in devotional exercises till within a few minutes of twelve o'clock. Then came a short interval of silence, when Mr. Knibb arose, pointed to the face of the clock, and exclaimed, "The hour is at hand, the monster is dying." There was stillness as of death while the clock struck out its twelve strokes, then Mr. Knibb exclaimed, " *The monster is dead, the negro is free.*" The people rose as one man, and broke into a loud and long continued burst of exultation. "Never," says Mr. Knibb, "did I hear such a sound, the winds of freedom

appeared to have been let loose, the very building shook at
the strange, yet sacred, joy. Oh, had my boy, my lovely,
slavery-hating boy, been there!" It was a terrible heart-ache
that his eldest son could not stand by his side on this day
of victory; without a son, to dedicate if not to sympathize,
he knew not how to exist, and in the supreme hour he
fetched his baby boy and held him in his arms in
the chapel.   The burst of exultation was followed by
three hearty cheers for the Queen, and by the singing of
a hymn.   The next day religious services were held
throughout the day, and in the evening a public meeting
was held at which all the speakers were descendants of
Africans, and acquitted themselves with credit.   Mr. Knibb,
in concluding, proposed a well-deserved vote of thanks to
Sir Lionel Smith, whom he justly designated as "the highly
esteemed Governor of this colony, and the ardent and
sincere friend of its enfranchised population."   The meeting universally rose in testifying their concurrence in this
vote.   In the evening the crowds retired to their homes.
Throughout the day not a drunken man had been seen
in Falmouth, and at its close scarcely was the voice of a
stranger heard in the streets.

The next day, the 2nd of August, was given up to making
the school children as happy as possible.   It began with a
procession of children made gay by a multitude of banners,
and headed by a carriage containing the children of
missionaries.   There were portraits for them of Clarkson,
Wilberforce, Buxton, and other friends of the negro, there
was feasting and singing and play, and they ended with
proposing "The Queen's health," "Peace and Prosperity to
Jamaica," and "Success to the good town of Falmouth"—all
given with "immense cheers."   The children dispersed
singing "We'll all go home together."

The outward and visible sign of something much deeper
is sometimes acceptable.   Those who knew Mr. Knibb

could hardly be surprised at a touch of the dramatic element amid the solemnities of the first day. A coffin was prepared, and in it were placed collar, chain, and whip—the emblems of slavery; the coffin was duly lowered into a grave, and the British Flag reared on the ground.

Without quoting the negroes' speeches at their public meeting, some sentences may be put down.

Mr. (they have been free some sixteen hours and they are all of them Mr. with a double name after it), Mr. Edward Barratt,—"We have been made to stand by and see our wives flogged, and we could not help them. The people of England did not see us, but God see us, and God stir up their hearts to get us freedom, and now we are all free people. Let us lift up our hearts and bless God, let us bless Queen Victoria."

Mr. George Prince-of-Wales,—"My dear friends, this is the day for us to rejoice. Walk upright. Remember it is your duty to support our pastor, his wife, and his children; if you do not support religion, you are not worthy of religion."

Mr. John White,—"The ladies in England expect to hear something good of us; we must try to behave ourselves as other ladies and gentlemen in this island do. Let us ask that Redeemer who sits on His throne, for grace to behave ourselves. Let us show the people in England that more sugar can be made by free ladies and gentlemen than was made by slaves. Let us be kind to our ladies. Let the friends in England hear something worthy of us."

Mr. Thomas Gardner,—"My dear brothers and sisters, now the black man can unite with the white; no distinction now, only of character. If any man will not behave himself, he is not free yet."

When he found himself detained longer than he expected*

---

* See letter to Mr. Abbot, Ch. V., p. 46.

in England, Mr. Knibb wrote a pastoral letter to his people.
In reading it, it should be remembered that the majority of
the people to whom it was addressed were at that time
slaves, and could neither read nor write. It is therefore
simple and short, without being childish.

"November 17th, 1833.

" MY DEAR FRIENDS,—

"Till within the last few days I had fondly hoped
that ere the receipt of this, I should have been among you,
for the purpose of again ministering to you in holy things.
Circumstances, however, render my stay in England for a
time necessary; and I therefore address this letter, that
you may hear of my welfare, and that in your reply my
heart may be comforted, by hearing that you are walking in
the fear of God, and in the comfort of the Holy Ghost.

" Though I have not received any direct communication
from you, it has rejoiced my soul to learn that you
have the ordinances of God's house once more as your
portion.

" Prize them highly, and endeavour to improve under
them. Let your prayers daily ascend to God, that He
would sanctify the Word to your souls, and to the conversion
of those who yet know not God, and who obey not the
Gospel of His Son. Most affectionately would I impress
upon you the duty and importance of prayer; without it
you can never thrive on the way to heaven; with it you are
sure of the blessing of God. Guard, I entreat you, against
falling out one with the other, and cultivate much the spirit
of love. Be anxious to attend the means of grace whenever
your duties will permit. Live near to Christ and heaven is
yours. Daily add to your faith virtue, and to virtue every
grace that adorns the Christian. I cannot exactly say when
I shall return, but I will inform you as early as I have
opportunity. The cause of my stay is on your account. It

is supposed that I shall be needed to appear before Parliament in the hope of procuring money to re-erect the chapels that have been destroyed ; therefore it is on your account that I remain. I do confidently hope that you will testify your love to me, and your gratitude for my exertions on your behalf, by frequently meeting to pray that God would bless my humble exertions, and restore me to you, in the fulness of the blessing of the Gospel of peace.

"I know it will please you to know that Mrs. Knibb and the children are in health. She often thinks of you, and prays for you, and it will afford her much pleasure if she finds that you all, and especially the female portion of the church, are living as becometh the children of God. Remember that when your religious privileges are granted you, God will expect much more from you. When you have more time to serve Him, He will expect more devotion to His cause. In all probability some of you will die before my return ; see to it, that I meet you with joy at the right hand of God. That will compensate for all our trials on earth.

"Daily do I think about you, daily do I pray for you. My happiness is bound up in your welfare. The knowledge that I am serving you in England makes me regret the less the separation I am constrained to endure ; and oh, may the God of all mercy grant, that when I do see you my heart may be gladdened by beholding your steady attachment to Jesus, and your daily attention to all His commands !

> "' Such is your faithful pastor's charge,
>   Whose soul desires not yours, but you ;
>   Oh! may he there, at God's right hand,
>   Himself and all his people view.'

"Let me hear soon of your welfare. Remember me to those country members who are not present when this is read, and tell them to watch and pray.

"That God in His infinite mercy may bless you, and bring you at length to His heavenly kingdom, that He may sanctify all your trials, and heighten all your joys, is the earnest prayer of

"Your very affectionate pastor,

"WILLIAM KNIBB."

Another letter is preserved, dated six months later, June, 1834, in which he tells them of the arrangement he had made with Mr. Dexter, and bespeaks for him their good-will.

"MY DEAR BELOVED FRIENDS,—

"Oh that I could fly on the wings of a dove and tell you the feelings of my heart ; but as this cannot be, I bless God that I can write to you.   By this time I suppose my beloved cousin, Rev. Benjamin Dexter, is with you, breaking to you the bread of life.   Let me entreat you to cheer his heart by your kindness, your steady attendance on his ministry, your consistent conduct, your zeal for God, your fervent prayers. Then he will be happy with you, and your God has done much for you, and may justly claim much from you.   Oh that there may be in each of you a heart to show forth His praise! My heart is pained, pained exceedingly at the many who have backslidden ; pray for them, pray for them, my dear people; speak to them, try to win them back to Jesus, so shall my heart rejoice even mine.   I wish I could say I had succeeded in procuring the money, but I do hope at length to be able to say it.   I hope to be able to tell you . . . that God has blessed my efforts and restored my health. You know there is a debt of £200 on the chapel (the one burnt down), I trust that you will try and raise this as soon as possible, that when I come I may instantly commence a new building.   I hope the deacons and members will assist all they can in the re-opening of the stations at Stewart town and Rio Bueno. Almost every day I am toiling for you, frequently I am praying for you. Pray for me, that I may be restored to you the sooner. I do wish that you would hold special meetings that God will direct me. That God may bless you, and that I may soon see you, and find you cheerfully obeying every law made for you by the Governor, is the earnest prayer of

"Your affectionate pastor,

"WILLIAM KNIBB."

CHAPTER VII.

TWO days, rejoicing, and then danger and difficulties. Mr. Knibb had been out for two or three days when at one of his stations—Waldensia—he received a letter of warning which made him hurry towards Falmouth. He was met by groups of armed men who had heard that he was to be hung. He persuaded them to give him their weapons, which were deposited in the carriage; nothing would induce them to leave him. Arriving in Falmouth it seemed generally known that an attempt would be made to hang him *in effigy* in front of the chapel. He found a magistrate at his house, who assured him that he had taken steps to prevent this scene coming off, and Mr. Knibb's volunteer guard were satisfied to depart home peaceably. There was no hanging, and no riot between his defenders and the other side—which, on investigation, it appeared had been reckoned on by some guilty parties, who intended foul play if the requisite confusion had only been brought about. The affair is told to Mr. Dyer as follows :—

"I know that an attempt was meditated for my murder, and had it not been for the firmness of Sir Lionel Smith, together with the determination of those who, though they have no religion, are attached to me, I should not now have been in the land of the living. I wish you distinctly to understand that I can prove that two magistrates were at the bottom of the hanging in effigy. My information is from a magistrate whose veracity is unimpeached. Besides this, a gentleman, who has sworn me to secrecy, has assured me that another magistrate told him that he knew a sum of money had been collected to assassinate me. In speaking to a magistrate only yesterday, he said: 'Mr. Knibb, it is nothing but their rank cowardice that has kept them from destroying you.' I know that it is the hand of Him Whose I am and Whom I love to serve. Fears I have none. My calm conviction is that I am in the path of duty, and that I cannot fall without the permission of Him Who has so often been my help and my stay."

Then came the vexation of erroneous versions of the affair in the papers—such as that he had entered Falmouth armed, at the head of an armed mob. He pointedly says, in reference to this, that he never had carried weapons at all, all through the disturbed time. The evil reports reached England, and, for the time, were in part believed; and admonitory letters, prompted by the Colonial Office, were sent out from Fen Court. It wounded Knibb deeply that the Jamaica papers had been believed as to this, and as to the conduct of some of his members.

Happily for the whole island, a cool head and firm hand were ruling. "The firmness of the Governor (Sir Lionel Smith) alone had prevented the effusion of blood."

Not among the least convincing to others, or the least gratifying to himself, of the proofs that the course he pursued was entitled to the approbation of right-minded men were the marks of kindness conferred upon him, in common with the Baptist missionaries at large, by the noble-minded Governor of Jamaica at that period.

In confirmation of this remark one example is given of the manner in which his Excellency was wont officially to express himself. In his reply to an address from the Baptist missionaries, met in their annual association in January, 1839, he said:—

"I shall say but little to you in regard to the calumnies of which you complain.

"Abuse is often honourable, and it has done great

service to your cause, for you may be assured it has extended the knowledge of your exertions, which have gained you ample honour in every other country.

" Had it not, and as long as I can give satisfaction to my country and my sovereign, I will gladly partake of that abuse, as a gratifying proof that we are fast destroying the last remnant of slavery throughout the world."

It is anticipating as to date, but this seems the best place to quote a letter of Mr. Knibb's written on Sir Lionel Smith's departure from the Island, October 1st, 1838.

" Our good old governor sailed yesterday, and I do hope that a hearty welcome awaits him at home. Richly does he merit all the esteem which the friends of the oppressed can show to him. His name will long be associated with the liberties of Jamaica. He has promised us his likeness, and we intend to have medals struck in silver, in bronze, and in metal, surrounded by his memorable answer to the government, in reply to the accusations of the planters that he wished the females not to work: 'I preferred the dictates of humanity to the policy of short-sighted planters.' I made the request for this when we presented our address, and he very promptly replied, ' Mr. Knibb, you shall have it.'"

To some the complete emancipation of the negro would have seemed the fulfilment of his labours. To Mr. Knibb it was the opening to fresh effort.

" I must establish more schools, and increase my native agency; I need, and must have, five or six more schools immediately, and I have the men and the rooms all ready.

" I long to extend operations here. The abolition of slavery has thrown the door wide open. The young men rising up rejoice my heart. Oh that God would still bless my humble efforts !

" The complete emancipation of the inhabitants of this colony has opened a glorious door for the extension of the Gospel in the interior of the island, which will very soon be peopled by those who will fly from the tyranny which will, in too many instances, be practised. Most of the labourers' grounds are on the borders, or in the heart, of these mountains, so that they are perfectly acquainted with the most advantageous spots, both as to fertility and water; while roads, at least passable, are in many instances made. Many have already either purchased or settled on lands, and I believe that I could now, if I had the means, purchase from 500 to 1,000 acres in one of the most lovely spots on earth, where scarcely human foot has trod, for about £2 or £3 sterling per acre. This I would purchase at once. I could soon re-sell to families in lots of from two or four acres each, which would enable the worthy members of my church, with others who are fearfully oppressed, to settle and form a village of their own.

"Of course, much, very much, remains to be done. We are only on the threshold of our work. The destruction of slavery has given us an open field, which we must labour to make 'as the garden of the Lord.'"

Every sentence describing one form of effort introduces some other sort of work, either consequent on, or necessary to, the carrying out of the first. Schools, for instance, are always insisted on. One can fancy Mr. Dyer looking on the Falmouth (Jamaica) post-mark and saying, "This means another school." And the schools wanted schoolmasters, and the schoolmasters themselves needed to be taught. These lines have the germ in them of Calabar College :—

"I look upon our schools as the grand lever by which we shall raise the people in intelligence, and the Gospel will then produce, I hope, in richer luxuriance all its precious fruits. One pleasing feature is that many of our young men are learning to read, and they attend regularly on the means of grace. More, I am confident, would learn to read had we a better supply of effective agency; this I hope our day-schools will soon afford. I hope also that from thence we shall have pastors for our churches, as well as masters for our schools, while benighted Africa shall by them hear the glad tidings of salvation.

"Two or three of my schoolmasters—natives—are daily increasing in piety; while I have others who, I am confident, under judicious training, might be made efficient in the Redeemer's cause. Now, if some of the wealthy disciples of Jesus would, for a year or two, take such persons—I mean by paying for their education, which could be easily attended to here—an immense blessing, at a comparatively trifling expense, would be conferred on the Church of Christ in Jamaica, and a native agency prepared, fitted to carry out that extension of the Gospel which is so much needed. Would not the Society patronise such a plan?

"My decided conviction is that the time is come for this to be tried, and my soul rejoices in it, and I write to you under the full impression that you will prayerfully take up the mighty subject, and have the happiness of laying the foundation of a permanent ministry in Jamaica. For some time I think it will be necessary for ministers from England to have the principal stations, as fathers to the church; and oh, may God, in His infinite mercy, spare those who are here, that the country stations may be thus supplied under their superintendence! But happy shall I be when even that can be with propriety withdrawn."

In respect to the relations with the Society at home, Mr. Knibb was bent on stirring up the native churches to support their own pastors and erect their own buildings, confining the assistance asked from England to extra efforts.

To Mr. Dyer—

" I sincerely hope and trust that most of the churches in Jamaica will support their pastors; if mine will not, I will not remain with them. I hope that next year I shall be completely out of debt, and that £100 sterling will be all that I shall require during the year to meet every expense. If I can do without this, you may depend upon it I will.

"I have now fourteen paid agents of the mission to support, besides myself and family; but the church is able to do it, and I am determined that, if possible, they shall do it. I must enlarge Waldensia immediately, but I do not want any assistance, though I know you would give it if I did, were it in your power. I merely wish to say for once that the chapels and other mission property have cost £9,000 sterling, that it is all paid, and that the chapels are all vested in the hands of trustees, and recorded in the Public Office in this island. I mention this lest any should suppose that the property is mine, a reflection which I should deeply feel."[*]

The natural healthy desire of the converted Africans in Jamaica was to take or send the Gospel to their Fatherland, of which more anon.

Socially the labour question was the leading one. For a few days after the 1st August, the negroes hung about, hardly knowing how to settle down, or on what terms. Then they had to come to some arrangement with the planters, who tried, many of them combining, to starve down the amount of wages to 6d. a day, with hut and allotment ground.

But negroes can count as well as dock-labourers and British miners. They had two points to start from : the money which had been paid from master to master when one hired out his slaves to another, and the prices charged to those who had wished to purchase themselves free at the beginning of the apprenticeship.

---

[*] Hinton's *Memoir of William Knibb*, p. 274.

Mr. E. D. Baynes writes to Lord Sligo : " Mr. Lord, of
Bowerwood, will not take less than 1s. 5d. per day—Mr.
Borrows less than 2s. a day—for common labour.   I find an
instance in the Parliamentary papers, in which a labourer
who had four years of his apprenticeship to purchase, was
appraised at the enormous sum of £166, which was two
shillings per day for every working-day comprehended in
the period.   Thus the value of labour was fixed by the
planters themselves."   Grant that this was an exceptional
negro of high value, still there is a vast difference between
two shillings a day and sixpence. " The people cannot live,"
said Mr Knibb, " on sixpence a day. This system will reduce
the whole labouring population to pauperism.   They shall
not accept of it." Mr. Knibb's plan was soon formed, and in
course of execution.   It was a counter-combination of the
apprentices, a universal and pledged determination not to
take less than so much ; the sum he proposed was one
shilling per day, with houses and provision grounds.   A
great outcry was made against " King Knibb, the monster,"
for interfering with the wages question, but in truth he was
no enemy to the planters, and helped them wherever he
could in making a fair bargain
  The proprietor of Oxford Estate, in defiance of the
sixpenny plot, offered one shilling sterling per day, and
requested Knibb to use his influence with the labourers to
accept of it   Knibb went to the estate, and had the
happiness of effecting the first agreement to labour made
after emancipation ; and when someone went among the
negroes in order to make them dissatisfied, by telling them
that their minister had made a bad bargain for them, he
went over again and said, "You have made the bargain,
and if you do not keep it I will never help you make
another."
  There were some proprietors who would not employ free
negroes and evicted them, pulling down their huts ; and

some masters for whom no free man would work. Jane Reid's husband, for instance, who had seen his wife put on the treadmill for not being strong enough for the day's task, and beaten by two men at once, could he have done a willing stroke of work for the master who ordered it, or taken his wage? Could he ever have respected himself, or could anyone else have respected him if he had?

For these people other work was to be found, and unoccupied spaces of land were bought, divided into allotments, and sold to the negroes, already accustomed to earn something by their provision grounds. Mr. Phillippo started the first of these villages, calling it Sligoville, after their good governor. Mr. Knibb bought and re-sold to the people three other sites.

How did the people while slaves get so much money? It seems that rations of bare necessaries were served out to them, but, in addition, they had each an allowance of ground. From this came all their comforts. They raised vegetables and poultry for themselves, and sold what they had to spare. It was common with those who were converted to set apart a fruit tree, or the eggs from one· particular hen, for the cause of the Lord.

The Jamaica papers were full of evil reports as to both missionaries and negroes. Their vituperation was let ·alone, but from time to time they made statements concerning individuals which had to be sifted and disproved. It is no use at this distance of time repeating these cases. The one of most importance as to the people engaged on the trial was the case of an English paper, the *John Bull*, which reprinted an article from a Jamaica paper. It came before Lord Denman the Attorney-General (Campbell) and Sir William Follett, with other lawyers, pleading for their respective clients, and some of the leading London merchants on the jury.

* " The trial took place at the Guildhall before a set of
London merchants, among whom were no less than three
West India merchants. I almost despaired of anything
more than nominal damages when I found the jury thus
constituted, all evidence of the falsehood of the libel
excluded, the tame address of Campbell, and the extremely
artful and powerful address of Follett. Nothing but the
honesty of Lord Denman and the high character of London
merchants (for there were some of the leading merchants on
that jury) saved the case. The court was crammed, and
the feeling was too strong to be got rid of by nominal
damages ; but there was an hour's fight for it between the
summing-up and the verdict.

" The result of such a verdict in such a court, between a
persecuted missionary and the recognised organ of the
planters abroad and the high church party at home, was
highly beneficial to Mr. Knibb in the scene of his labours.
He was deeply grateful for it, and I believe to the day of
his death felt his obligation for the trouble, expense, and
anxiety with which I pursued, and ultimately achieved, his
vindication."

These social questions were enough to fill the hands
of a very energetic man. Mr. Knibb might have added,
" Besides that which cometh on me daily," the superintendence of "three stations with a population of 16,000 persons,
four male and four female teachers, seventy people con-
ducting prayer-meetings in seventy different estates, thirty
deacons, and twenty Sabbath-school teachers."

---

* Statement of Henry Wait Hall, of Bristol, who undertook to carry
the case through.

CHAPTER VIII.

VISIT TO ENGLAND, 1840.

AT the beginning of the year 1840 it became desirable, for several reasons, that the Jamaica Mission should have a spokesman in England. His fellow missionaries deputed Mr. Knibb as their representative at the approaching Anti-slavery Convention. There were other matters of importance—more missionaries were greatly desired; so were the means of training native ministers and schoolmasters on the spot. Besides, the African negro churches in Jamaica, undertaking the support of their own pastors, earnestly hoped that the London Committee would organise a mission to their fatherland, and they wanted this claim enforced.

And then there were the evil reports. There was a planter-party in England, as well as in Jamaica. There were, too, irreligious people always ready to believe anything against a convert; and, besides all this—much of which they could have afforded to disregard—were the doubts of really good people as to whether the mission was being wisely carried on, and whose fears were fanned by the representations of two Jamaica ministers of other denominations, who disapproved the methods of the Baptist missionaries. This last circumstance grieved Mr. Knibb deeply, for he had worked hard with one of them, trying to keep the people quiet in the disturbed New Year of 1832; and the other had been on "such brotherly terms with him." He conquered them both, as a Christian should, by a personal interview, going over the matter as reasonably as possible. The result he tells to Mr. Dyer

It is highly characteristic of the generous nature of the writer :

" It will afford you pleasure," says Mr. Knibb, "to learn that I have had an interview with Mr. Blyth ; that we have agreed to forgive and forget all past differences, and to act as brethren in future. We knelt at the throne of mercy, and prayed, each of us, with and for each other. I go this week to assist in his church in the formation of a branch Bible society. May the Lord bless the union to the advancement of His glory ! "

And with regard to the second : " Immediately on the receipt of yours I copied the extract referring to Mr. Vine, and sent it by express to Arcadia, together with a note expressive of my regret at the circumstances to which it referred. To it I received a kind reply, and subsequently I had an interview with Mr. Vine, whom I highly esteem, when he left the impression upon my mind that nothing was further from his intention than to cast a slur upon the whole of our churches , that his remarks were intended to be confined to Arcadia ; and that not knowing members of our churches he could not thus have designated the whole."

The two brethren themselves were conquered for the time, but the reports had given an uneasy feeling to the churches in England ; not the animosity of an enemy, but the ultra conscientiousness of a friend—a friend who believes you mean right, but are not working in just the right way.

In those days it was supposed that a Baptist church in Jamaica should be exactly like a Baptist church in England. Perhaps they read about being "very jealous for the Lord of Hosts " oftener than they read "diversities of gifts, but the same spirit," and feared the West Indian stations were going astray. The *good* people at home wanted to know if communion tickets were not an evil. They were not in use at home then as they are now ; it was contrary to our customs. The *enemy* went much further, declaring that they were purchased by those who would, without regard to character; others that they were held in superstitious awe as charms.*

Other doubts formulated themselves into questions such as these: Did not the very largeness of the churches show that sufficient care was not taken.in admitting the members? Then, is it not making Methodists of them to have classes, and class-leaders? Were not the leaders often unfit persons, ignorant, and loving rule and authority?

This system of classes had been formed to meet the circumstance that the Christian negroes were scattered over many estates, and that it was desirable to have some-one on each estate who could look a little after the rest. Mr. Knibb speaks of seventy prayer-meetings on seventy different estates. These leaders were ignorant, which at that time they could not help. Whoever has been under the tender mercies of the darkey porter of an American hotel will surmise that they could be authoritative; but they were chosen as true-hearted men, and dismissed if it was found they were exerting their influence wrongly. Then, were not the missionaries luxurious? They kept horses, while the village pastor in England went afoot; they ate turtle, while he ate bread and cheese.†

"In Jamaica," reported Dr. Angus at Exeter Hall, after

---

* *Hinton's Memoirs of William Knibb*, 207. "Respecting the value the negroes place upon the tickets, I have asked Mandingo, Guinea, Eboe, and Creole slaves; I have also sent the most intelligent of the members to inquire on the remote estates, and I have not yet discovered one instance where any superstitious regard is paid to them. Indeed, the slaves consider themselves insulted when you ask them the question. 'Do you think we are such fools as this?' they reply."

† Some years after the writer asked Mr. Knibb's daughter—married, and in the thick of housekeeping—what was the price of turtle? The answer was, "6d. the pound, the same as other meat."

being in the West Indies, "turtle is the economy, and bread and cheese the expense," the natural products being cheap there, while imported over here they are a great luxury at a high price.

Without the horses it was explained the out-stations must be left to themselves, and the little knots of people already spoken of, to the ignorance of the native class-leader. Mr. Phillippo could minister at Kingston, Mr. Burchell at Montego Bay; but to look after stations and schools eight, ten, eleven miles off could only be done by constant travelling, in a tropical climate, and where there were no public conveyances. Hence the horse, the alternative being another white missionary at every station

Again, the number of church members was a stumbling-block. People read happy accounts of large churches they did not see, and therefore did not realise the number of careless godless people in the district, or calculate the large spaces from which the one church was drawn. The missionary on the spot could contrast his 2,000 members, attendants and school children, with the 20,000 living without God in the world, and feel the work was only beginning. And this again enforced the cry for more men. Geographically, all these large churches might well have been divided into two or three, each with its own pastor, But where were the men?

So with all these questions to answer as best he might, Mr. Knibb set forward on his voyage to England. He had his own two daughters with him, his cousin, Mrs. Dendy, and her son, with two black members of his church in his charge as well. The sea voyage in a sailing ship is a change of subject, and details are ventured on :—

To his wife.

"At Sea, off the Island of Cuba.

"*31st March,* 1840.

"My dear Mary,

"When I shall finish this depends much upon the weather. Hitherto we have been placed in such trying circumstances that I knew not that I should ever write to you again ; but we have had to sing of mercy as well as of judgment, and a kind and powerful Father has appeared for our succour. You will have learned by my last from Kingston that we were obliged to return to Port Royal, the vessel having sprung a leak. We again set sail on the Friday following, and all appeared ready for a prosperous voyage.

"On Saturday morning the alarming sound, 'Breakers ahead!' was heard, and as the sun had not shone for two days, and a strong current was running, we knew not exactly where we were. However, these we weathered in safety, and all appeared right; but the same evening, when I was looking for a psalm to read, and the dear children were preparing for bed, the vessel struck upon a reef, going full seven miles an hour at the time.

"Oh, it was a serious time! I had all the children dressed, commended them to God, and went on deck to see what could be done. There lay the vessel on a bed of hard sand, surrounded by rocks, on which the waves dashed and foamed.

"During the night she pitched heavily, and I feared she would go to pieces. But God was there. The wind lulled, and our opinion soon was, that she would lie till morning. The dear girls expressed a humble hope in the blood of Jesus, and soon fell fast asleep. Dear little William (Dendy) said with great simplicity, 'Not my will, but Thine be done,' and then he, too, fell fast asleep. I sat up with Mrs. Dendy all night, or nearly so, and I think we both felt

6

the value of an interest in Christ, and a good hope through grace of eternal life.

" Towards morning the ship rolled heavily, and we longed for the break of day that we might attempt something for our rescue, having secured a change of linen, should we be obliged to leave by the boats. The captain sent out a small anchor, to see if the vessel would wear off, but the ground was so bad that it would not hold.

" The only hope left was in throwing the cargo overboard, and all hands at once commenced. I think I never worked harder in my life.* About half-past four, Sabbath evening, our efforts were crowned with success ; she floated, a breeze sprung up in the right quarter just at the same moment, and in a few minutes the vessel was in deep water.

" Though we had been on the bank for twenty-two hours she had not sprung a leak. We had to throw over about five thousand pounds' worth of coffee and preserves, and other materials of which the cargo was composed. We had not got off more than three hours when the wind shifted and blew half a gale, so that had we not succeeded when we did, as far as human supposition can go, we must have been a complete wreck. Thus again has life been preserved, and I hope it will be for the glory of God.

" A very kind kiss to the little Africans (two children that he had taken out of a slave ship), a kind message to Charlotte and Nellie, tell them to walk in the fear of God, and then happiness is assured. Let George know that I am interested in his welfare, and I hope that he will train up his children in the nurture and admonition of the Lord."

(There is a note in Mrs. Knibb's handwriting, written across the letter to explain that Charlotte and Nellie were their servants. Nellie was an old African who had been

---

* " Either *prayed* harder or *worked* harder," he writes to a cousin.

with Mr. Mann, and lived with the Knibbs to a good old age. George, too, had lived with Mr. Mann and grown up in the family, and was, at the date of this letter, a class-leader, and very useful in the church.)

" May 2nd.—We are still on board the vessel, with a foul wind. It is rather a gloomy aspect : our food is nearly all consumed, the children's clothes are nearly all torn or dirty, and patience has not yet her perfect work. At our family prayer-meeting the children have read with myself and Mrs. Dendy, and we have thus gone through the Psalms. The children have very generally repeated a hymn and a verse of Scripture, which I hope they will remember when they are separated from both of us."

To the same.

" Liverpool, May 10th.—I left the ship, in company with Mrs. Dendy and the children, at Holyhead, about sixty miles from Liverpool. It was calm, and yet with every prospect of a foul wind, and our provisions were nearly exhausted. We found out Mr. Morgan, the Baptist minister, and were soon comfortably housed at an inn kept by a Wesleyan sister. It would have delighted your heart to see how the children made the bread-and-butter disappear. It really did my heart good to see them so happy. And then, how the folks did stare, and the children jabber ! Surely Babel was not more confounded than we were. Nobody spoke English except the dogs. We went round the town to see the churchyard, the meeting-house ; then to the abode of an aged female disciple—ninety years has been her pilgrimage. Her cottage was the picture of humble neatness. Let me see—there sat the fine tortoise-shell cat close to the fire, which quietly consumed itself for our benefit. The two old arm-chairs would have spoken if they could, and told of the wonders of the last century. The best set of fire-irons, polished like a mirror, were posted on a small wainscot, which separated a small room used by the rev. divine as a study, in which were a chair, a table, and a candlestick, with portraits from the *Baptist Magazine* of some of the worthies. Then the bright copper warming-pan, the smoke-jack laid up in ordinary, and all the implements of enlarged cookery, arranged with the precision of a toy-shop, and as clean as labour could make them, gave the extended mantelpiece a most inviting appearance. The other parts of the room were in perfect harmony; indeed, a crockery shop could not have displayed more taste. It was necessary that everything should be in its place, for there was no room for it anywhere else. Well, there we are seated—cannot you see us ? The good old body stirring up the fire, and shutting out every breath of air. She talks of the poor slaves, rejoices that they are now free, when all of a sudden out comes a volume of real Welsh. Oh, that you had been there to interpret it, and to assist in drinking, in a glass of the days of George I., some of her choicest raspberry cordial, which I suppose was kept for special visitors ! She was a lovely Christian, and assured us with simplicity that she never went to bed without praying for the missionaries. The next morning we started at five, and all nature was dressed in loveliness ; the mounting lark (which sang in English) sweetly warbled the praises of its Maker ; the blossom of the may-bush sent forth its fragrance ; the corn sprang up in its freshness, and the shrubs and the trees were clothed with leaves, while the blossom of the apple and other fruit trees assured us that there was not only beauty but plenty in store for man. We sang mother's favourite hymn, as Kate calls it, ' Guide me, O thou great Jehovah '; and after a pleasant ride of twenty-three miles we came to the Menai bridge, the most wonderful structure I ever beheld. There we took a steamer, which in six hours safely brought us to Liverpool."

Mr. Morgan, the Baptist Minister of Holyhead, reported that Mr. Knibb seemed to have no great taste for ecclesiastical antiquities, as he failed to take much notice of the Parish Church, thirteen centuries old. An attempt to get into fellowship with the aged Welsh sister by trying to sing the Old Hundredth together—he in English, she in Welsh —likewise failed; never mind, it was a wonderfully happy morning. The brightness deepened into thankfulness, when some days afterwards, May 10th, the ship they had left dragged herself into Liverpool harbour, having encountered a severe gale, lost part of her bowsprit, and with only a few biscuits and a little salt pork left in the way of provisions.

He and his party were warmly received at Liverpool.

His feelings as to his appointed work during this visit to England find expression in a letter to Mr. Dendy, dated May 2nd.

"Of course, I am all in the dark respecting my future movements, and I hourly feel that I need much prayer to keep me from disputing God's will, or murmuring at His dispensations. Oh, that He may sanctify me thoroughly, and in some humble measure fit me for the awfully important mission on which I am sent! That mission rises daily in importance in my mind, and I hope that all my beloved brethren will bring it frequently before the churches over which they preside, and be earnest at the throne of grace for the promised blessing."

Mr. Knibb had been eagerly expected for the annual meeting of the Society, for which the contrary winds had made him too late. He had, however, so much that was important and interesting to tell, that an extra meeting was convened at Exeter Hall to welcome him and hear his statements.

He took one point after another.

The export of sugar was less? True, but then more was

used in the Colony, and other things, which had been kept out for the sake of the sugar crops, were now being cultivated for the use of the inhabitants.

"The negroes were idle." On this point he says: "I delight in being able to read the testimony of an esteemed brother with whom I was once at variance on the subject of emancipation, the Rev. George Blyth, on this point. He says, 'Instead of accusing the labourers of indolence I am rather disposed to blame them for being too anxious to make money. I do not know a healthy person in the congregation who can justly be called idle.' There are many circumstances contributing to the diminution of colonial produce. If the planters choose to risk their property in the hands of idle men, I ask that you should blame the right persons. I should like to know if any farmer in England could go to a dance, to the opera, employ one person at £500 per year, another at £300, and others at £70, to attend to his grounds, and then expect more than 100 per cent.? There is no soil in the world can do it, and Jamaica cannot do it.

"We have determined to prevent pauperism if we can. Among the lately emancipated negroes there is not a pauper in connection with our churches in Jamaica, and I have no doubt the same may be said of the churches of my esteemed brethren of other denominations. In the parish in which I reside, it was asserted at the last vestry meeting that since the abolition of slavery the poor rates had been doubled. I knew the inference that was intended to be drawn from this. I went to a vestryman, to whom I said, 'You have told us part of the truth, now tell me the whole. How many blacks who were once slaves are there among the paupers?' What was the reply! 'Oh, not one.'

"The improvement of society is to be seen in the diminution of crime. In my own parish, containing 30,000 individuals, only one person was tried at the last assizes.

Mr. J. J. Gurney visited the gaol, and found one person in it—*a white man*. In the parish of St. Ann's the gaol has been shut up for six months.

"The women are kept at home whenever the men can afford it. We have 5,203 children in the day-schools; 645 in the evening-schools; 9,159 in the Sabbath-schools, and other denominations are as successful as ourselves."

Part of the speech was on the question of missions to Africa, in advocating which Mr. Knibb said he had come in the name of 50,000 Baptists who want their fatherland to receive the Gospel. "I met some of the Africans of the churches of Kingston before I left. One of them said, 'I will go as your shoeblack if you will take me.' 'When will you be ready to go?' 'To-morrow,' was the reply. I said to them, 'Perhaps you would be made slaves again if you were to go.' What was their answer? 'We have been made slaves for men, we can be made slaves for Christ; these are the men that ought to go.'"

Before launching into his long speech he had introduced his two negro fellow travellers, Barrett and Beckford. It was Beckford's province to go steadily to a normal school and qualify as teacher. Barrett, a much older man, went about a good deal with Mr. Knibb. He had a touching story. Some years before he had, while a slave, rendered some public service, for which the House of Assembly gave him his freedom. He thanked them, but said he was growing an old man and had not many years to enjoy it, would they confer the freedom on his son. They did so, and the generous old father remained a slave till the abolition set every one free.*

Mr. Knibb had something else with him which sent a thrill through his audience, the spiked collar and manacles which, if memory serves right, one of these men had worn.

---

* This is from memory, the vivid memory of early impressions thoroughly believed to be correct.

Having shown them, he threw them down on the floor of the hall, amid such a burst of excitement as made one young auditor at least thoroughly frightened, thinking the building would give way.

After the public meeting came the business meeting with the committee, when he entered with them into the two objects on his heart: the appointment of additional missionaries to Jamaica, and the commencement of a mission to Western Africa. Both points he carried as to intention, promising to go himself about the country as soon as freed from the Anti-Slavery Convention, which he had come over to attend, and stir up the churches for the right men and the means, while the theory of the African mission had to be shaped into practical working order. The first step was to send out two pioneers, Rev. John Clarke and Dr. Prince, who reached Fernando Po, January 1st, 1841.

The fact that he was away from his wife gives us the advantage of his numerous letters, written to her very much in scraps of time and carried from one place to another till the sheet got full. The following is selected because it is in fact, though not in form, the journal of a week, and, with the exception of the Anti-Slavery Convention (to sit the next week), all his interests seem mentioned—wife, children, station, false reports, additional missionaries, money (not copied), Africa, Committee of the House of Commons, travellings often, weary waiting for the information he wanted for the Colonial Office—all compressed into one closely written quarto sheet :—

"Ipswich,
"*July 5th*, 1840.

"My beloved Mary,

"I am anxiously awaiting the arrival of the packet, which I hope will convey tidings of your welfare. My heart so yearns over the church and station that I can scarcely get on at times with the important duties I have to perform. To-day I have to preach three times in this place, but I seize a few spare moments to hold converse with you, whom distance makes doubly dear to my heart. Oh, that I could tell you all I do feel on this subject, but it is needless; soon I hope to be able, not with pen and ink, but in sweet intercourse, to hold fellowship with you. Since I last wrote I have been incessantly travelling and holding meetings on behalf of Africa, and in every place the Lord has given me favour, so that a deep interest is excited on behalf of degraded Ethiopians. Three missionaries* are already accepted for Jamaica, and two others will be in a short time. I cannot do any more in female education till I hear from Jamaica. Many more offers (such as are good) have already been made than can be accepted."

Details follow about one pair of these new missionaries to be sent off quickly, and received, if she thinks fit, by Mrs. Knibb The sheet is taken up again next day—" I sent out to Br. Dendy by last mail a copy of a letter I had received from the Colonial Office respecting the laws of Jamaica. I have *since heard* that they will not be allowed unless much altered. I do hope we shall at length succeed, though the tide is evidently very much against us.

"Tell Mr. Dendy that I think petitions sent home from the peasantry would do good. I fight on as best I can.

"The subject of native agency is much canvassed now by all denominations, and will be attended to by all. I hope, therefore, our litle academy will not go to the ground, and that the scheme of female education will meet the attention it deserves.

"I go this morning to breakfast with the venerable

* Some of the ten that he had pleaded for earnestly with the Committee, and for whose expenses he was collecting, as well as for the proposed African Mission.

Clarkson, after which I proceed to a public meeting at Diss, and another at Bury. I shall be sincerely thankful when the time comes for my return. I do not wish at all to be repining, as I humbly hope God is making some use of me to promote the Kingdom of His Son. Oh, how happy should we be could we always live near to Him and devoted to His blessed cause!"

"London, Friday.—I came up from Ipswich to appear before a Committee of the House of Commons.

"I am exceedingly anxious that the Jamaica mail should arrive, as the false reports of the meeting at Falmouth are doing harm. . . . I am doing the best I can for the people, but it is wearying up here" [waiting for the desired information].

More details about the sailing of Mr. and Mrs. Henderson, about the children, and movements to and fro.

"Norwich, Sabbath morning.—'Hail, blessed day!' Oh, that it may indeed be blessed to our souls and those of the Church! Tell the deacons a very kind 'howdee,' and tell the leaders to give my love to all the people, and to beg them to pray much for me and for one another. The claims of Africa wake the deepest interest."

A later letter, 14th August, reports: "Travelling all night, and the West Indian mail leaving this evening. Not a line to Jamaica written, and many things to write about," besides the pleasure of writing to his wife. He finds time for a sentence about Bristol—next to Kettering, the place of his early affections: "It is very much altered, especially the Kingsdown and the places most familiar to us—houses, and new street close by the house where you used to live. I did feel a sacred joy in thinking of bygone days in the few minutes I had to spare for visiting that part. I have seen Miss Spurrier," &c.

The letter closes with messages, the remembrances he always made time for: "Give my love to the dear children

—to the people. Tell them to pray for me, and to live near to God. To George: I am glad he is so attentive to the Africans—may they be the Lord's; to old Nelly and Charlotte; to the deacons; yea, to all, for my soul yearns for their salvation."

A few weeks later, October 4th, he can write, "Well, now for the news, I have taken my passage in the *Reserve,* and expect she will sail at latest by the 5th of November. I write thus early that our friends may remember us in their supplications."

The later letters, among lists of places where he had been or had still to go, have in them three pleasures that came to him. Mr. Clarke, "dear Clarke," and Dr. Prince really started for the West Coast of Africa, so the much-longed-for African Mission might be reckoned as begun; he had had an interview with Joseph John Gurney, of Norwich, "whose 'Letters on the West Indies' are just printed, and will do immense good;" and the last and nearest to his heart, a letter from his own Catherine. "Dear father, when do you think I may be baptized, for I long to be a partaker of the Lord's Supper. I thought how it would rejoice your heart to see me a child of God. Oh, that I were more like my blessed Saviour, more meek, holy, and submissive to my heavenly Father's will! My thoughts followed dear Mr. Clarke, and I hope he will succeed in his mission. My fervent prayers accompany him."

So much copied the father with a hand unsteady for very joy, for the mother's heart to share in the purest parental joy that Christian parents know. Our children are not quite ours till they are God's children, too.

Mr. Knibb summarized his work during his visit thus—

" When I look at the results of my mission in England, I am both thankful and humble. Oh, what a condescending Being must God be to employ such an instrument in

His service ! I have been in England scarcely five months' and now there is every reason to expect that the laws in Jamaica will be altered ; the African mission has been commenced ; eight missionaries have been accepted by the Society out of the ten for Jamaica ; within a few pounds the money has been raised for their passage and outfit ; and I have every prospect, if health is continued by the blessing of God, of raising the remaining sum required, and of finding the men by the time I have engaged to leave. Oh, this is a mercy, and God shall have all the glory ! How 1 desire that a successful blow may be aimed against American slavery, and that it may fall, all bloody as it is, before the cross of the Redeemer."

CHAPTER IX.

ENGLAND, 1842.

SOME delay, owing to damage done in rough weather while the *Reserve* was still in the Thames, put the voyage off to November 16th, when Mr. Knibb sailed with some of the new missionaries he had entreated for, and some ladies who were to take up the cause of female education on the island—a party of fifteen in all. They landed on January 7th, at Rio Bueno, receiving an enthusiastic welcome. Very glad was Mr. Knibb to be with his own people again. A public meeting to welcome him on the 12th January was followed on the 19th of February by a missionary meeting on behalf of Africa, so crowded that an overflow meeting was opened in the Suffield Schoolroom. After these came large Baptisms. Following one of them, the churches of Falmouth, Refuge, and Waldensia united in observing the Lord's Supper, when the communicants filled the large chapel.

So much has been said from time to time about careless admissions to the church, that it may not be out of place to quote Mr. Knibb's charge to the newly baptized.

"You have now all solemnly declared to us that you have felt sincere repentance towards God on account of your sins, and that you have fled for refuge to the Lord Jesus Christ as the only Saviour of sinners; and on this profession you have this morning been baptized in His name, and are now about to be received into communion with the Church. Did my time and strength allow, I should now offer you a few words of Christian caution and entreaty; but it is not needful. You have often been assured by my lips that without holiness not one of you shall see the Lord. Let it be yours, then, most earnestly to seek after holiness, to manifest the temper of Jesus Christ, so that at last you may be received by Him, and sit down with all the sanctified in heaven.

" It remains for me now only to give you, in the name of this church, the right hand of Christian fellowship. With that hand you will receive a heart that longs most intensely for your salvation, and your entire conformity to the will of God. In the name of this church I welcome you among us, and may every blessing ever rest upon you ! "

Before the distribution of the Lord's Supper Mr. Knibb had said, " I am sorry, very sorry, that those who are not members must now withdraw. My dear fellow sinners, there will be room enough for you in heaven. Jesus is ready to receive you, and the church will welcome you."

Let us get a glimpse at what was to the negroes the festival of the year, the 1st of August, a day of gladness and faithful remembrance of the Lord's mercy, but not now at this date, 1841, of such strong excitement. The custom seems to have been for the mission family to go round to the different stations as far as possible, and Mrs. Knibb writes to her daughters :—

" KETTERING,

" *August* 27*th,* 1841.

" You will see in the *Herald* an account of our August meetings. They were very pleasant, as they generally have been in bygone days, and much, very much, were you talked of by your father and myself, and often have we wished you had been going the usual round with us.

"We had one or two more places to visit this year than we used to have when you were with us. At Unity the first post of a new chapel was stuck in the earth (it is to be built of wood), under the scorching rays of an afternoon sun ; there were about 1,000 persons present. It would have highly amused and pleased you to see how amply the poor people had provided for us; three or four fowls, boiled or roasted, a pig, yam, and although we were none of us hungry, we were obliged to try and eat a little, lest the friends should feel disappointed, after having taken so much trouble. So I sat down on the grass under the shade of a mango tree, and took the fowls in my lap, to cut up and hand round to the friends of our party. From thence we went on to Waldensia, where Mr. and Mrs. Cornford joined us and spent with us the remainder of the week."

Then the tone of the letter changes from its easy gossip, to detail a summons at midnight to go to Mrs. Cornford, who was very ill. "We never could have thought that our cheerful, happy friend would in less than a week be numbered with the dead. We all feel it much, and you will feel it, too, for she loved you both, and was often talking about you. Oh, the infinite value of that hope which supports the mind in a dying hour, and enables her sorrowing friends to look through the gloom by which such a scene is surrounded to the brightness of those pleasures which our dear friend is enjoying !"

As it throws a light on Mr. and Mrs. Knibb's character not yet shown in this Memoir, part of a letter from Mr. Cornford is quoted here. He says: "Not a sacrifice has seemed too great for them (Mr. and Mrs. Knibb) to make. They came to us at midnight, when first they heard of our woe. They tried every means to supply our wants. They closed the eyes of my dying wife ; they took me from the awful scene to their own home, where I have since been cared for as an only child. I am supplied with all that affection could suggest or heart desire."

About this date there arose another battle to be fought for philanthropic ends. This time it was on behalf of the Irish immigrants, who had been persuaded to come by those planters who wished to supersede the negroes. These poor creatures for the most part sickened, the climate did not suit them, nor the food, nor work under a tropical sun. Mr. Knibb comforted some, buried a good many, and, as he had done in bad cases among the slaves, sent affidavits of special hardness straight to the Governor, Sir Charles Metcalfe. Mr. Hinton prints some of the letters received in answer, with money assistance for the sick, and for paying the passage home again. A commission was instituted. Some of the evidence taken was too ugly to publish, and was suppressed. Mr. Knibb gave over a copy he obtained to the Anti-Slavery Society.

It was very trying to have the same dissatisfaction re-appearing, with the conduct of the mission that has been spoken of in pages 77-9, charges of too luxurious life, to be met as to food by the market prices ; as to the horses and carriages, by the distances to be travelled constantly without any public conveyance,* and the worst and most prominent suggestion, as to the purity of the churches and the appointment of leaders at the out-stations, always a sore question. We need not repeat many of the details ; though in testimony to Mr. Knibb's own character, we must remember that he waded through it all again, being deputed by his fellow missionaries to represent them in England. It was very distasteful to him to leave the people and the work he loved. For their sakes and the brother missionaries' sakes he did it.

He had requested of the accusers the names of any of

---

* NOTE.—Mr. East says :—" In former years, and at the time of my leaving Jamaica, the cost of a journey from Kingston to Mount Carey, near Montego Bay, and back, with your own buggy and horses, including a needed rest for the night on the road, was £6. The usual charge of a livery stable for the same journey, one way, was £10 or £12. Since the extension of the railway, the same distance may be travelled in four hours and a half at a cost of five shillings each way."

his own members who might be in fault. The Western
Association of Baptist Churches in Jamaica put forth a
printed list of all the deacons and office-bearers in their
district, and asked for specific charges against any of them,
could such be brought. No instance in either case was
brought.

Question had been made as to the accounts of the
Society, and for this he gave as referees Messrs. J. J.
Gurney, Sturge, and Candler, members of the Society of
Friends, who had recently visited the island. One episode
under this head is very interesting, and it is not a repetition
of detail to quote it from Mr. Knibb's speech : " It has
been said that the Baptist missionaries dare not publish
their accounts ; if they did, the Baptist Mission would be
ruined. Very well, I will publish mine." And forthwith
came the charges for chapels (built to replace those burnt
down in 1832), school-houses, fences, furniture, and one
£50 for taxes—" the last that we have to pay, for so
complete is the change that has come over the spirit of
our dreams, that (it is with the greatest pleasure I state
it) the opposition has spent itself. The House of Assembly
has, unsolicited, passed a law relieving missionaries of
all denominations from every public and parochial tax
whatever."

" When I laid this report before the members of my
church — of the chapels out of debt, and vested in
trustees—and when they found that the very furniture
of the minister's house was theirs, not mine, they said :
' Minister, have you took good care and got a home for
your wife ? ' ' No ; do you think I would take your money,
without your leave, and buy a house for Mrs. Knibb ? '
' If you have not got one, it is time you had. Go to
Kettering, and, on the land that is not yet taken up for
allotments, build a good house, and we will pay for it.' I
took them at their word, for one of them, Edward Barratt,

said : ' You may die, and we cannot bear the thought that
your wife should go home ; let her stop here.' I built
the house—it cost £1,000—and assigned it over to Mrs.
Knibb and our dear children, determined not to hold any
property myself.   Mrs. Knibb is in it now."

He went on to say the people had built their own
prayer-houses, sixty of them, where in the villages class
meetings and prayer-meetings are held.   These did not
enter into the accounts he had given of the sums furnished
and expended.

The opinion of the Society at home is thus recorded in
their report for the year 1842 : " In churches so large
and so scattered as those of Jamaica, where there are a
thousand members to each missionary, and nearly as many
inquirers, it will readily be seen, that much of the success
of the pastor must depend on the co-operation of the
members of the church.   This co-operation most of our
brethren enjoy.   The churches are generally divided
into districts according to their localities.   These districts
meet weekly or oftener, for prayer and religious intercourse.
The more intelligent and pious of the members preside,
and are expected to report the state of their districts from
time to time to the pastor.   The same plan is adopted in
reference to inquirers, and thus by judicial distribution
of labour a much larger number of persons have the
benefits of religious training than could possibly reach
them by other means.   The results of these labours the
committee have carefully watched for several years, and
they are constrained to believe that they are such as
deserve the support and ought to awaken the gratitude
of their friends."

Mr. Henderson, who was one of the young missionaries
first selected by Mr. Knibb in his visit in 1840, went to the
Falmouth group of stations till Mr. Knibb's return, settling
at Waldensia. Of course, he was on the missionary side,

but he may be worth quoting as fresh from England and quite fresh to negro workers and class-leaders.

He says, " I have no reason to suppose that the deacons at Waldensia are better than those at Falmouth or at Refuge, so that when I tell you that at Waldensia I find in the deacons and leaders a band of devoted pious men, who are willing to give anything for the cause of God, I wish you to understand that I am not singular, but that my brethren are surrounded with those who are quite as devoted, and quite as well-informed, as those who surround me, and without whom I could not do one-third of what I am now able to accomplish."

CHAPTER X.

THE visit of Mr. Knibb to England, which is the subject of the previous chapter, synchronized with the Jubilee meetings of the Baptist Missionary Society. Among his own letters to Jamaica, there is only one page as to the part he took in the celebration at Kettering, dated on the Sunday following from Liverpool, June, 1842 :—

"MY DEAR MARY,—This is a day of rest, and I have come hither in the hope of enjoying a quiet Sabbath. It has been a most bustling week—the Jubilee week at Kettering, some account of which I must try to give you, full details you will have in the *Patriot*. I took the dear girls, who much enjoyed it. . . . I preached twice at Northampton on the Sabbath, and we had a public breakfast on the Monday morning. We returned to Kettering later in the day. The town presented a scene of activity and joy fully in accordance with the object for which we were assembled.

"I think that from 8,000 to 10,000 persons were present at the different meetings. On the Wednesday evening I had to give three addresses—at the Baptist Chapel, at the Independent, and at the tent, which held more than 4,000 persons, so that I was about two and a half hours speaking. Public breakfast, 500 strong or more, next morning. Collections, £1,300. I went the same day to Birmingham, and on the following held a public meeting in the Town Hall. Mr. James proposed a vote of confidence in my brethren, and I was presented with a silver medal, which I hope to show you by the 1st of August."

And then the letter goes off to other subjects. Mrs. Knibb must content herself with the newspapers for all fuller accounts of the Jubilee meetings till they meet and talk.

Those who remember this commemoration, remember how he was the special attraction; how people would not settle down in the overflow meetings without the assurance that he would come and speak there, too. The writer has seen a letter from an ardent young girl who was present. It is deliciously fresh and enthusiastic. The exquisite delight on finding that her railway ticket (numbered in those days to one particular seat) took her into the very carriage in which her hero was travelling, how fatherly he was, how the multitude impressed her, how the interest settled on *him*, and then how at the refreshments provided afterwards he was as busy as other mortals seeing that the ladies were seated, and provided with food. Is it not written for the benefit of the school friend who could not go?

Does anyone say "The words of a gushing girl!" The fathers and mothers of these enthusiastic children who understood better what had been accomplished were no whit behind them in eager feeling. For it was not the *man* only that so made them rejoice. It was the victory that he had won, that *they* had won. The slave was free all over British dominions; and in the West Indies, wherever evangelization had gone, the negro had stood the overpowering excitement well, and had not broken out into wild lawlessness; which is the more wonderful as all through, the religious slaves were the minority, but for all that with influence to leaven the majority.

But all the while Mr. Knibb's heart was set on getting back. "I hope to reach Kingston by the 27th of July," he writes on the 24th of May. "I do not wish that you should come any way to meet me. I write this because of some joking remarks I made last time, but I had much rather our meeting took place in our own lovely home, when prayer shall ascend to the Author of all our mercies.

"And now, my dear Mary, join your husband in praise. Ere this reaches you I fully expect to have baptized our dear Catherine. She is a lovely, but timid Christian, and when she opened her heart to me it was almost too much for me to bear. She dates her conversion to the grounding of the vessel on the shoal at the commencement of the voyage home 1840."*

A letter in June says, "Yesterday I baptized our beloved Catherine and six others at Salem Chapel, Brixton, and after the evening service, when I preached to a crowded audience on 'Occupy till I come,' I admitted them into the church."

As on the voyage to England he had written constantly to his wife, so on the voyage out he wrote by every opportunity to the daughters he had left. They were letters full of observation as to natural objects, and references to the history of the places where the vessel touched, advising them to refer to books and maps and get up the subject well.

Any modern travel-book would give the same details, the point here is, that the letters show so plainly that God was helping His servant, as He does many others, by the sight of His mountains and trees and bright rivers, by His calm face of ocean, or "stormy wind fulfilling His word." So the voyages and journeys were good gifts from the Father, refreshing soul as well as body for hard work and burdensome anxieties.

Among the many manuscript letters of this sort was one precious letter to Ann on spiritual matters.

---

* Chap. VIII., p 81.

"ON BOARD SHIP,

"OFF MADEIRA,

"*July 9th,* 1842.

" MY DEAR ANN,—I employ a few minutes with much pleasure in writing to my own dear girl about that blessed Jesus whom I hope she loves, and to whom I pray her life may be entirely devoted, and I hope ere long to hear that you are the decided follower of the blessed Saviour. Your dear sister Catherine has openly avowed that love to Christ which I would fain hope you feel, and to His willing arms I invite you to fly, assured that He will pardon every sin, conquer every corruption, receive you graciously, and love you freely. You, with your dear sister, will, I expect, ere this reaches you, be thinking of returning to school, after having enjoyed the holidays there new duties will await you, new mercies be granted to you, and you will need the aid of Jesus that you may rightly perform the one, and daily improve the other. You have now youth upon your side with all its manifold advantages of serving God. Oh, then now, my dear girl, approach His mercy and live—live for God, live to God on earth as the sure and certain hope, and the only one through the blood of Christ of living with God in heaven ! I feel happy that I shall have to tell your dear mother how much gratified I was with the general conduct of both my dear girls, and I hope by constant perseverance you will both soon obtain that knowledge which will fit you to return and live with us ; but you will both have to work hard to accomplish this, and I hope you will daily strive so to advance, that your industry and advancement may appear unto all. But *more than all,* as of the last importance, watch, strive, and pray against sin, against *all* sin. Make the Saviour your daily companion, His word your law, His commands your delight; then will happiness be your portion, God your friend, and heaven your home.

"Prayer will be your daily solace and your daily joy if you are truly the child of God—private prayer, social prayer, and public prayer, when in the house of God you meet to worship His great name; and let me remind you not to forget your relations, your parents, and especially the perishing heathen. Cultivate, both of you, a missionary spirit; so that, should it please God to return you to Jamaica, you may be deeply imbued with the spirit of the work in which I hope you will be through life engaged. I fear I shall not be in Jamaica by the 1st of August, but am hoping for the first Sabbath in that month, which will be peculiarly gratifying to me. We have had more favourable weather; the sun smiles, and the wind is light, but fair.

"And now, my dear girls, farewell. May the God of your mother be your God, and your portion for ever."

A few lines, written after he was at home again, speak of their coming home to help, as he hopes, in his work :—

"It ever gives me pleasure to hear of your welfare. . . . I am looking forward . . . to the period when you will be able to return to Jamaica. You must work hard, my own girls, so that the time may not be lengthened.

"The Jubilee Meetings have been well attended, and have, I hope, done much good."

An extract from a letter recently written by a niece of Mr. Knibb's will help to throw light on what sort of father was waiting for his daughters to come home. This lady arrived in Jamaica the last day of 1844. Her uncle died November, 1845, and part of the time he was away in England. So she says :

"I had not many opportunities of seeing him or knowing much of him. I was fourteen when I came to Jamaica, and with him I counted among the children, and he was always happy amongst them. My recollections of him are all happy, but they are all the recollections of childhood. One that is very distinct is seeing him in the pulpit, giving out, 'Stand up, and bless the Lord.' His voice was singularly sweet and clear, and I never read that hymn or think of it without having a vivid picture of him before me."

It has not seemed a violation of confidence to write as openly as this of the two dear daughters. No secret of theirs is betrayed; it is all the tenderness of the father's heart to them, and these two, as well as the others, have long been with him in the "Father's house on high." While speaking of his love to children, it seems best to anticipate a few months, and quote from a letter written to his wife in July of the following year, during her visit to England :—

"It is dull enough here, as there is no child, nothing but the horses, dogs, and fowls, and the stately mother peahen, who will, I think, rear her brood.

"The dear girls you will see. Fanny will be all alive. The little cherubs in heaven will be happy in their joy, and we will bless God that we have five safely landed in that blessed abode. To the dear children a father's kiss and a father's blessing; to yourself all you can desire in time and eternity."

After thus counting his treasures, who can wonder at the next extract (July 20th)?—"I preached last evening from 'The whole family in heaven.'" It is a delightful subject. *In that family there are an innumerable company of children* —that was one of the divisions.

His love of children was thus commented on by a friend in England :—

"He was passionately fond of children, who always reciprocated his love; and he used his influence with them for their highest good. I have seen him gambol with the

little ones on the floor, and, when he had won their hearts
by his sympathy with them in their childish sports, he
would place them on his knees, and, kissing them, he
would then talk to them of their Saviour's love to children,
till the unbidden tears trickled down their cheeks.   So
completely did he fascinate them, that they were less
willing that he should cease his conversation than they
had been just before to finish their play.   They clung to
him yet more closely, and, if they were less merry, they
were more happy.   I believe that the fruits of righteous-
ness which are now found in many of the young in our
churches may be traced to some heavenly seed which, on
such occasions, he deposited in their hearts."

Another person remarked : "I can understand almost
everything Mr. Knibb does of a public nature, but I
have been surprised to see him enter so deeply into the
amusements of his own and other people's children—a man
with such a weight of cares and so many public duties."

Mr. Knibb arrived at home on the 4th of August, and
found his family in health and his church in peace.

The people of the Western Union had already decided
on a celebration of the Missionary Jubilee in Jamaica, to
be held on the 5th and 6th of October.   Fresh from the
Kettering meetings in England, Mr. Knibb threw himself
heartily into the preparations.   It was no small undertaking
to form a sort of camp where 12,000 human beings and
2,000 horses could be kept for several days.   One most
gratifying part of the preparation was that the planters, by
their managers, rendered most essential aid—so had the
state of feeling changed in ten years.   For the negroes,
who were unfit, as they then said, for anything but coercion,
and whose religion they persecuted, and for the man they
wished hung, they were now volunteering kindly service,
which Mr. Knibb acknowledged most heartily in one of
the meetings.

There were three days of the meetings—"a feast and a good day" might be said of them in the spiritual sense—and everything [that could be done was done to make them bright. The captain of a merchantman in the harbour lent his flags; the overseers from the neighbouring estates, as before stated, did very essential service : the children sang; the platform had on it many spectators, magistrates and others, to watch the proceedings and carry away their impressions ; and at the end of the time the Lord's Supper was partaken of by about 4,000 communicants. There would have been another day of meeting if the food supplies of the village had held out, but some had, perforce, to return home. Mr. Knibb left the scene to go to other meetings. " I seem to have about a month of it before me," he says.

And then, in less than six months, what had happened before, in the midst of success and popularity, happened again—a very severe private sorrow.

Of four sons, only one was surviving—the child whom he had held as an infant in his arms on the night of the Emancipation, and who was developing like the tenderly loved and remembered William.

On Saturday, the 18th of March, he seemed quite well in the morning; a little ailing later in the day; ill all day Sunday ; Monday morning he died in his mother's arms.

They laid him in the same grave as his brothers, William and Thomas. The father controlled himself to write submissively, but very sadly, to his daughters in England. His letter to Dr. Angus breaks down with—"I would write more, but I have no heart for anything ; the loss of my only son presses me heavily to the dust, for he was a lovely boy."

No wonder that to such a man the house was "dull enough, as there is no child *here* "; no wonder that, in his anticipation of heaven, "an innumerable company of *children are there.*"

CHAPTER XI.

IT became evident early in 1843, that what had only been talked of the year before must be accomplished this year—complete change and rest for Mrs. Knibb.

She started in May, on board the *Hopewell*, with her youngest daughter.

Mr. Knibb's letters during this period of separation furnish us with a better account of his usual home work than has been given yet. They will not be quoted entire because so full of detail, but extracts, or sometimes mere tables of contents, are valuable as showing his varied and incessant occupations, and the extent to which his wife, his Queen Consort and Queen Regent, fondly loved and tenderly cared for, was in all his confidence sharing his burdens as well as his joys, with the freedom of thought and action which he gave freely, and which contributed largely to her usefulness.

" The enlargement of the chapel at Waldensia has been completed, and a very interesting meeting held in commemoration of the event. This week I am going, as you are aware, to Coultart Grove, taking Kettering and Brown's Town as preaching places in my way.

" The congregation at Falmouth was better yesterday*

---

* It was Mr. Knibb's principle never to suffer the church under his care to become very large. He much preferred the formation of new churches in suitable neighbourhoods. Acting on this plan, his church at Falmouth underwent an amicable division no less than six times, several hundred members being dismissed on each occasion ; and when he saw the chapel partially empty, he said cheerfully, " We must work hard to fill it again."

than I have seen it for some time, and I hope that the steps taken to promote a revival will have the desired effect."

"To-day —— has applied to be received into the theological institution, so that I must make arrangements for the supply of his place.

"The premises at * Calabar are progressing very rapidly, and I hope that by August matters will be in a fair way for a thoroughly good commencement. Six candidates have been accepted.

"This evening we have a special prayer-meeting on behalf of the South Sea Mission, which appears in great jeopardy. Well; 'The Lord reigneth; let the earth rejoice, let the multitude of the islands be glad thereof.'

"I have my fears that this will prove a sickly year, and we as a mission cannot expect altogether to escape. Well, it is all in the hands of a faithful God, and He, you know, my dearest girl, will do all things well. We have the most abundant cause to trust Him. For twenty years He has mercifully helped us, and we have the hope of a happy for ever."

"At present I bear my temporary widowhood with exemplary patience, though, by the bye, nobody else has discovered the fact."

"I hope that you will make your mind quite easy on the score of expense. What there is to be seen in London, see it, and do not work too hard. I expect, if practicable, you will visit in many places; but do not fatigue yourself, and be sure to use your cash on omnibuses and railways."

"We are all in the enjoyment of health and heat, and the mosquitoes are regular attendants at Chapel."

The letter of July 1st must remain a silent witness, the affairs it speaks of are over, and the people dead; but it just

---

* The Trust deed provided not only for the education of Ministers, but schoolmasters. A normal school as well as a "Theological Institution."

shows how he made Mrs. Knibb partaker and councillor in everything that was going on, the awkward things no less than the smooth.   It ends, " The people are already inquiring whether I have heard of you. Some of them designated you by the title of ' Mother,' not at all an inappropriate one."

"The packet is in.   No letter from the girls Quite busy—quite well."

July 12th.—He discusses : Friendly societies for mutual relief in sickness among the people; the condition religiously of the neighbouring islands ; paying a visit to Boston, America, at the invitation of the Anti-Slavery Society there ; and then turns to commissions to be executed in England, and domestic matters.   The good folks " tell you how-dee."

July 20th.—Mentions the sermon about the innumerable company of children in heaven already quoted.

July 27th.—Home affairs, the garden, especially a certain bread-fruit tree, fowls and little pigs ; day-schools, Sunday-schools, hoping that his daughters would take up the one at Refuge.   Then an instantaneous photograph ; "—— is much as usual, full of whims and of piety "

Again (the same month, day not legible).   Enjoy yourself as much as you can, and use all the means that are desirable for the recovery of your health.   As you will naturally suppose, I am following you in all your tracks."

A very grateful and gratifying notice follows the resolution the committee had passed to pay Mrs. Knibb's expenses, though he would like to consult her before accepting it.

Mention is made of the home—her favourite plants and animals

" I received an interesting letter from St. Domingo. There is a chapel and a church, and a minister much wanted ; leave I cannot, except some help is sent ; yet the call is very urgent."

"Our dear Coultart's image is almost ever present when at Kettering. Fanny (with her mother in England) I miss much. But it is all right."

August 4th, is taken up with the 1st of August anniversaries.

August 13th, with news of various people; some discouragements; commissions; an appeal about taxation; an opportunity of buying more land to be sold in small portions to cottagers; the new Kettering village is forming nicely.

September 3rd, tells of an attack of fever. He believes he shall be *quite well* by the time the letter has to be posted. It is like some others written journal-wise, a piece each day. "I should not have said anything about the sickness, but your confidence would have been shaken had you heard of it from others. I wish you to be as happy as you can. Make yourself quite comfortable about me. I am safe and happy in the hands of Jesus, nor will He leave nor forsake me.

"The day this sheet begins to travel, I shall have attained my fortieth year. So is my life flying away. Oh, that I may have the call to work while it is called to-day— to be the active servant of the adored Saviour !"

Perhaps he was too anxious to prove himself "quite well" the day the mail went, and hurried into work again, for on the 10th he has to confess to a relapse, through exposure he supposes, and in the enforced retirement records his thoughts, instead of his doings and his surroundings. "I feel, and long to feel it more, that salvation is all of grace. Oh, what a mixture of vanity and unworthiness does a review of life present! What an unspeakable mercy that the precious blood of Jesus Christ cleanseth from all sin, and that none are excluded from a full participation in the benefits it confers! I think I can say that I had rather endure sickness than commit sin, and that I do pant for more conformity to God. I know not what hope any one can entertain from anything he has done or can do. Were it not for the Atonement I should sink into despair; but 'it is a faithful saying, and it is worthy of all acceptation, that Jesus Christ came into the world to save sinners.'

"I know the deep anxiety you will feel, combined with the fruitless wish that you had been here, and right glad should I have been had Providence so ordered it; but friends have been very kind and attentive, and I hope that, long ere the packet sails, I shall be about my accustomed duties. You will remember, my dear, that *I have told you all. I have not been at all worse than I have said*, and I do not at present see any reason to think that I shall be. I mention this that your mind may be quite easy on this matter. You have often committed me to the care of my Father, and He has heard and answered your prayers."

And there is a joyous ring in the sentence towards the end of the letter, that it is the last but one he shall have to write.

The Calabar Institution has been mentioned several times in these letters, Mr. Knibb having more to do with the preparation of it than he would have had if it had not been for the serious illness of Mr. Tinson, who was to conduct it.

The last letter of the 1843 series is an affectionate note to Mr. Tinson, on his having safely passed through a serious operation, summing up with, "Now I shall enjoy a happy Christmas."

He had another reason for a happy Christmas. He had got his wife and daughters safe home.

These extracts have been given to convey some slight idea of the variety of a West Indian missionary's duties. The following from a letter to W. B. Gurney, Esq., enforces this view of his life:—" . . . It has more than once suggested itself to my mind that you are not fully sensible of the very different position we occupy from that of ministers at home. Here we are obliged to be everything—everything religiously, politically, civilly, and (if I may coin a word) *buildingly.* While our brethren at home have deacons who can manage the temporal affairs of the church, and collect the necessary moneys, we must be responsible for all, and manage all. While at home there are laymen to whom the poor can go for advice, and even for legal advice, here ours is the only appeal. Every disagreement, domestic or civil, comes before us ; by our advice they go to law, or by our advice, abstain. It is just the same in political matters ; not a step will they take, nor an agreement will they sign, without asking us. Often have I had persons come to me for advice who have walked twenty miles to ask it. All their titles are brought to us to see if they are right, and the knowledge that this will be done prevents many attempts at gross oppression. Thus, after the morning is past, a missionary (perhaps more especially myself) is not sure of an hour. Now, what are we to do in such a case ? "

There is among the letters one with a defaced date, in which he speaks of being at Kingston, having "preached three times on the Sunday, and does not feel quite well, perhaps, *because he has not enough to do.*"

The next point of interest was the arrival of the *Chilmark,* with Mr. Clarke—chartered to take over to Africa such Jamaica coloured brethren as he, with the concurrence of the resident ministers thought fit for missionary work in their fatherland.

The plan was not quite in accordance with Mr. Knibb's judgment. He wanted these people to have had more training, certainly, to have been at Calabar; if possible a year in England; but when his idea was overruled, he entered heartily into the speeding of these new pilgrims

8

and under due superintendence steered the ship out of harbour.

They were, especially to him, an interesting group, these men and women who were returning free to the countries from which they had been carried'away slaves. One among them had been taught to read by William, the beloved son ; one Mr. Knibb had trained himself; one was the superintendent of his own Sunday-school, and another had only just lost his wife, who dying, had begged him not to give up the cause they had meant to work in together.

The most familiar to us in England is the Rev. J. J. Fuller, grown grey in the service, a lad then, going in the *Chilmark* to join his father.

CHAPTER XII.

ENGLAND FOR THE LAST TIME.

ABOUT this period the affairs of the mission generally became very difficult, through several causes which operated to produce a great scarcity of resources.

In the very large outlay required by the erection of so many chapels, considerable sums had been borrowed from the banks, then very willing, if not eager, to advance them. Circumstances now forced them to restrict, and in some cases to recall, their advances. A severe drought lasting over two seasons added to the pecuniary pressure on the estates, and reduced the peasantry on their small allotments almost to starvation.

There is the prettiest picture in the April number of the *Missionary Herald*, for 1844, of a neatly-planned village of cottages (not one of Mr. Knibb's stations), mountains around, trees nearer in tropical luxuriance, and a distant view of the sea, a delightful home for people well-to-do in a small way; but, turning the leaf, one reads of the bitter distress brought by the dearth. Those inhabitants who had nothing else than their bit of ground saw their only subsistence perishing before their eyes. From living sufficiently well, and being able to devote their fruit or their eggs as a fund for giving away, they had very hard work to provide bare necessaries, and hardly dare think how to keep or buy seed for the next year's planting.

So that when island banks or private persons lending money on the chapels could not prolong their loans, it was no time to go to the people for extra gifts; they were

8*

suffering themselves, and could hardly bring their usual offerings.

They had undertaken at the time of the Jubilee the support, independently of the Society, of their ministers and stations, with a tacit understanding that the Society should undertake some African stations, which arrangement had been carried out.

This was possibly a premature measure on the part of the weaker stations, and those still encumbered with debt. The larger stations were equal to the burden; Falmouth, for instance, had paid its way—chapel, schoolrooms, minister's house all paid for—yet even Falmouth was in straits about its schools. Mr. Knibb writes:—" We are grievously distressed by the severe drought we have experienced, and the effect upon our mission and schools is most trying. I have struggled hard to support four day and four Sabbath-schools at an expense of £400 per annum, but shall be obliged to relinquish part of them, which will grieve me to the soul. I do not like to ask help from home, yet our schools are our only hope."

Another trouble at Falmouth was one which could not have affected that place alone. We have the same thing in England, when we see a good chapel in the midst of a town almost deserted because its members are gone to reside in the suburbs. Mr. Knibb took an opportunity of buying an eligible piece of land near enough to keep some of his people within touch of the chapel, but the hiving off had been very heavy. It was promoted at first, but became a difficulty as the years went on, and more and more people turned their faces towards the mountains. But if his chapel at Falmouth was not in debt, he was responsible to a certain extent for others. He had hung a weight round his neck. In his own words: " Some years ago I very foolishly became surety for -——— and for ———. I had not the least idea but that they would long ere this have paid the bank all they owed. In this I have been dis-appointed, and I am resolved, let the consequences be as they may, to get rid of these responsibilities. I entered on them purely that the brethren might not draw on your funds which otherwise must have been done."

There had never yet been a year in which the buoyant spirit had been so bowed down—the pilgrim's road was heavy and stony, the hope, the determination to succeed are absent for the first time. It wrung from him, what wicked men plotting his life had never wrung, such a sentence as this, "Sometimes I think I will leave altogether." It may be added that the Government of the island was, in his opinion, going the way to ruin it. Also the Mission Com-mittee at home having to refuse many of the requests which seemed to them endless, appeared cold to the strugglers on the stations.

In this state of things he was requested by the brethren again to visit England, and lay their case before the Com-mittee. He agreed, and sailed the end of March, 1845. From sea he wrote (on April 15th, 1845) to his daughters, now in Jamaica with their mother, a letter as to the help they might give :

"Your dear mother has had a hard and sometimes painful path to tread. Added to her maternal cares and the bitter pain endured in the loss of our dear children, she has borne much of the anxiety of the stations under your father's care, and I fear her health is declining. I assure you, my dear girls, that I attribute most of my success in my missionary career to your excellent mother. The accumulated duties and increased anxieties pressing on your mother during my absence will afford you the luxury of showing how much you sympathise with her ; and thus, should I be permitted to return to my dear family, the meeting will be doubly endeared to you, and to us all, by sweet reflection on duty performed."

He arrived in London towards the close of April, and met the Committee on the 26th of that month. They received him with undiminished cordiality, and entered into the consideration of the case entrusted to him in a spirit perfectly congenial with his own.

He himself states the case most clearly and in fewest words, as follows : " My dear Mary,—While I am waiting for my turn to speak at the chapel, I write a few lines, just to say a little about the meeting. The Committee resolved, and the public have agreed to it, that we shall have £6,000 as a gift to help in our difficulties, but they will not take any station under their care. Nothing is to be drawn until my return, when the whole matter will be laid before the brethren, and the approval of three-fourths of the whole will be necessary to the validity of the matter."

" I wish to leave it deeply impressed upon the minds of this Christian auditory, that nothing could have exceeded the kindness and the urbanity of the Committee in all the transactions in which I am engaged with them   I undertook the office which I executed with extreme reluctance ; I would not have come on it if I could have avoided it, until stern duty forced upon me this employ-ment, no arguments would have induced me to forsake the beloved people of my charge and the endearments of social life, to come home on what I consider one of the most unwelcome errands on which it was possible to send a man. I have, however, been most agreeably disappointed ; I have been affectionately welcomed, not only by the Committee, but wherever I have gone, and at the simple tale of wrong, the guilty doings of the men that have brought us into this condition, there has been, not merely an approval of what the Committee has done, but a hearty response as far as pecuniary aid could be given."

He spent two months in England, holding meetings as often as he could, to assist by his powerful eloquence in

raising the money. This money question was not, however, the only question. At these and the Anti-Slavery
Society meetings he strove to make his audience conscious
how some of the island laws weighed unjustly against the
free negro. There were taxes framed to load him heavily
while the white man went nearly free, and disabilities which
were remnants of the slaveholding spirit. Such were the
Ejectment Act and the Trespass Act. By the first the whole
population, or any portion of it, could be ejected at a week's
notice from the homes in which they had been born; by
the other "the police of the country was empowered to
catch hold of and imprison any individual who was found
in his former home, after he had received notice of ejectment." They were miserable cabins, these slave huts, with
eight or ten persons huddled into one room, yet it was beyond
all reason to suppose that the negroes would improve huts
from which they could be turned out at a week's notice.
This led the peasants to secure if they possibly could a
home for themselves. " It has pleased our heavenly Father,"
he continues, "to afflict us with one of the most severe
and long - continued droughts that I have ever known
in Jamaica during the twenty-one years of my residence
there. The House of Assembly selected this period,
when they knew the peasant could not obtain work
to introduce a new tariff. An additional tax was laid
upon the wood which the labourer had to purchase that he
might erect his own cottage ; which raised it from 1s. per
1,000 shingles to eight; the food was also taxed ; when the
planter had to feed the slave, the tax on cornmeal was 3d.
a barrel ; as soon as the freeman had to feed himself they
raised it to 3s.; rice in the same way was raised from 1s.
per cwt. to 4s. Other articles were mentioned, and then
the speaker turned to the grievance of an expensive mounted
police in "peaceful Jamaica," so quiet that the mail
carrying thousands of pounds has travelled with only a

negro boy, and has never been robbed but once, and that by a white man; and increased rates were levied on behalf of the established Church, "established" only by courtesy.

In a later part of the speech Mr. Knibb goes into the statistics of the Baptist mission as they stood at that date. There were forty-seven Baptist chapels and thirty mission-houses, besides the schoolhouses, costing altogether £157,000, of which, with much difficulty and much diligence on the part of the people, £139,000 was paid off; the remainder in a time of scarcity, and with new taxes laid on, was a crushing load, to ease which the sum of £6,000, already spoken of, had been granted by the Mission Committee in England, and which Mr. Knibb was up and down the country to help them collect as an extra effort.

CHAPTER XIII.

"IT IS ALL RIGHT."

THE kindness with which Mr. Knibb had been received and the success granted to his errand, touched him deeply and in most warm-hearted terms he returns thanks for it over and over again.

"I felt much more in leaving England this time than I ever felt, I know not why, but so it is. The kindness received has been far beyond my merits."

None the less was his longing for his home in the Island and for his work there. The depression was gone, there is no more talk of wishing he could see his way clear to leave altogether. He has taken his passage for Kingston which he hopes to reach July 31st. Will Mrs. Knibb send the gig and the horses off in good time, that they may rest well and be fresh? George is to travel slowly and arrive at Kingston the 29th. The large horse is to be left at St. Ann's Bay, apparently for relay. No one but George is to meet him, that he may have a light load. He will land and make a dash for Falmouth, driving all night to be with his people on the 1st of August.

With all this good will, he can hardly be said to have won the race, for he did not get home till the evening of the day which completed seven years of freedom. An ecstatic meeting it was for all that. For the people kept the next day as a festival, forming a long procession, which Mr. Knibb longed for his English friends to see. "How I wish —— and —— and —— were here," he kept saying, as he watched its progress.

And then the regular work began again, increased by the business entailed by his last visit to England.

It may not be amiss to copy here his estimates of the stations he had formed, as he gave them in England on this last visit.

It should be premised that when he first went to the west of the island, the whole of Trelawney was reckoned as his district.

The population of it was 30,000, the area an irregular square about twenty miles long, and from seventeen to twenty broad; the stations six, eight, ten miles apart, Stewart Town and Rio Bueno about eighteen from one another in opposite directions from Falmouth, with no public conveyances.

When I went to Falmouth in 1830 (succeeding Mr. Mann), I found the station without a house, without a school, and without a schoolroom. The first house I lived in there had but one room in it, ten feet square, for six of us. I had been there but a year before down came all the wrath of the slave-owners upon us. Chapels were destroyed. . . . Since that time there have been erected the following chapels :—Falmouth Chapel, which seats 2,500 people; Refuge Chapel I built next, which seats 1,500 persons; Rio Bueno, seating 1,000 persons; and Waldensia, which seats 1,200 persons. Unity and Stewart-town Chapels have been built by other brethren, one holding 600 and the other 1,200 people. Last year I repaired and made comfortable a chapel at Kettering (one of the free villages), it holds 400 persons. Thus there have been erected in ten years, chapels for the accommodation of nearly 8,000 persons.

At the time of which I speak, there was no schoolroom at all in Trelawney to which a black child could be admitted; there stand now in connection with our own mission, seven or eight. Then, the only room which the

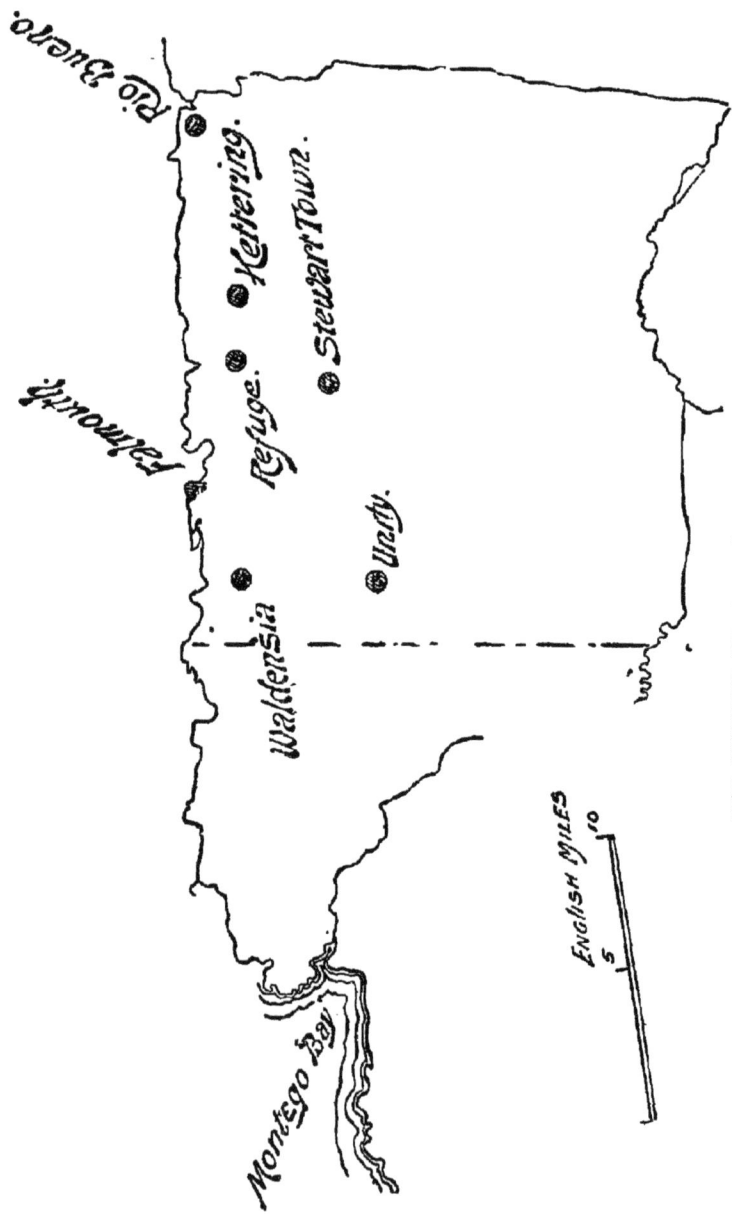

MAP SHEWING MR. KNIBB'S STATIONS.

missionary had was the one to which I referred, now there are five or six dwelling-houses in healthy situations.

Then I had 650 members. From that time down to the present I have, by baptism, assisted sometimes by other brethren, received into the church, 3,000 persons. I have dismissed to form other churches, 2,050; there have died in the faith 320, and as far as I can make out, after a careful examination of the church books, only a hundred have been put away. I will tell you how the numbers now stand: Falmouth, the mother church, is mine, 1,280 Refuge, our eldest child, 780; Rio Bueno, 315; Waldensia, 746; Stewart Town, 814; Unity, 340; and Kettering the newest, has 200 members.

Rio Bueno was by this time under Mr. Tinson's care; Stewart Town under Mr. Dexter; Mr. Henderson had been for some years pastor at Waldensia, to which Unity was added; while Mr. Knibb retained Falmouth, Refuge, and the new village station Kettering which he was fostering.

The map gives Falmouth, Rio Bueno, and the stations Mr. Knibb founded in the Trelawney District. In the fifty years that have elapsed since his death, eight more have been added, "all," Mr. East says, "the extension and outcome of Mr. Knibb's work." The total member-ship at the present date is 4,397, with 640 inquirers.

They say, "Coming events cast their shadow before." Is it not true that coming glory sends some rays of light before? Men took knowledge of the apostles that they had been with Jesus! His friends took knowledge of Mr. Knibb that his spirituality had increased; there was something of the other world resting on him, as well as the eagerness to do all the good he could in this world.

"It was evident to all our friends," says Mrs. Knibb,

"and especially to myself, long before his last illness, that he was rapidly growing in meetness for the inheritance of the saints in light; he was so earnest in pleading with sinners, so mild and faithful in reproving those who he thought did not live up to their high profession and privileges, and so animated and heavenly minded at the ordinance of the Lord's Supper, that although I enjoyed the services, I used to fear there was too much of heaven in them for him to be long an inhabitant of earth."

Not that any change was apprehended; he laid the foundation-stone of a cottage for one of the people, saying, "Tell your neighbours I will do the same for them when they are ready." His attendance on meetings, his list of engagements, remained unabated; he was not trying to save his "iron frame" though some short fits of illness might have been taken as a warning.

Mr. Abbott gives his account of a Sabbath—November 9th—spent at Falmouth with him. "At six o'clock a.m. we walked together to the house of God, and both engaged at the prayer-meeting. At eleven o'clock he baptized forty-two persons and was unusually touching and solemn in his remarks to each. At the close of the meeting I preached from John vi. 29, and, a short time after, we unitedly administered the Supper of our Lord. He had published that I would preach in the evening also, but, having recently suffered from an attack of influenza, I begged to be excused, with which he kindly complied, and preached himself—his last sermon—from 1 Tim. i. 2: 'The glorious Gospel of the blessed God,' or, as he delighted to say, 'The Gospel of the *happy* God.' On his return from chapel I sat with him about an hour, when at my request he recapitulated the leading particulars of the sermon. I have spent many days with our sainted brother, but I do not remember ever to have spent one more happily. He was in a calm, solemn, equable, happy frame of mind, and

he remarked to me that he had been more pleased with his
people that day than at any previous time since his return
from England."

But he had taken a chill. In a profuse perspiration
from preaching, he had walked home in the rain without overcoat and umbrella. On Monday, Mrs. Knibb
thought him over-weary after Sunday's duties, though
he had come from Falmouth to Kettering cheerfully
enough.

The low fever of the earlier days became the yellow
fever by Friday. Family and friends were round him
watching with most anxious care. Mr. Abbott lingered, so
did Mr. Burchell who had come into Falmouth on business,
—these were his fellow-sufferers in all the troublous times,
the latter keeping such close vigil that he did not undress
during the days that followed. The sufferer as is usual in
the low typhoid fever of the first days, was disinclined to
speak much, and while the least hope remained was kept as
quiet as possible. He did not hope for himself, and spoke
of a speedy decease to Mrs. Knibb and the elder daughters;
expressing also to his brethren his faith in the Atonement as
his one hope of salvation. His farewell to Mr. Phillippo
was full of affectionate concern for the trying circumstances
in which the latter was placed.

He said to his daughters, "My poor girls, you will soon
be fatherless; live near to God by prayer and work for Him.
Do all you can to keep up the schools. And mind you
take care of your poor mother. She has had an anxious
trying life and often rough path; and she will need all the
sympathy and tenderness you can show her."

With the development of yellow fever came delirium, first
shown by his giving out a hymn, and setting the tune as if
for a large congregation. The hymn was followed by a connected and most beautiful prayer. He had no long interval
of consciousness afterwards, but in one clear moment he

stretched out his hand to Mrs. Knibb and said, "Mary, it is all right." They were his last words.

And so, on Saturday the 15th November, 1845, the news spread rapidly among the people he had loved so well: "Massa Knibb dead."

"And they lifted up their voices and wept."

His last Sunday service on his visit to England, so short a time before, had been at Denmark Place Chapel, Camberwell.

Once before when he had been there, there had been a special farewell communion service. It was said that he was disappointed when he found that he was expected to preach. At the distance of nearly fifty years that service is well kept in mind by some few who remain.

"We both remember the service you inquire about and often speak of it to each other." So runs the answer to a question put to two old members of Denmark Place Chapel.

The text was "Son, go work to-day in my vineyard;" and the work God appoints His servants is giving the message of that other last sermon, at Falmouth; "the glorious Gospel of the blessed God."

It is the summing up of his own life.

After that sermon at Camberwell, he gave out as the closing hymn,

"What must it be to dwell above,"

and charged all present to meet him in heaven. It sounded as he gave it like no vague benevolent wish, but as a definite appointment.

Some of us who remain to this present, are going on our way to "keep tryst."

MRS. KNIBB.

CHAPTER XIV.

A BABY daughter, Mary, had died in the early Port Royal years, William, the twin brother, died as a boy old enough for many hopes to be concentrated upon him. Three other sons died at a still earlier age, five out of the innumerable company of children in heaven, that he speaks of. Three daughters were living at the time of their father's decease. The elder ones, the Kate and Annie of the letters, married; the youngest of the flock died after a long and painful illness, borne with Christian patience of hope, and nursed devotedly by her mother.

It was after this daughter's death that Mrs. Knibb again visited England, in 1863, to the great pleasure of her friends.

And this sketch is hardly complete without the record of the peaceful death of the noble wife, as told by her daughter in Jamaica, Mrs. Fray, in a private letter to a friend in England :—

"April 23rd, 1866.

"It is with a very sad heart that I write to let you know that my beloved mother has entered into rest.

"For a long time she had been gradually sinking, but we hoped that she might be spared to us yet a little longer. Our heavenly Father called her home a little after midnight on the 1st of April. Her sufferings were very great for the last few days, till within a few hours of her death, when all pain was removed. Early in the morning she said to me, 'There is a land where it is always Sunday, and I am not

very far from that land now.' During the day she often
repeated, 'I will come again and receive you to Myself.'
Once we heard her say, 'Nothing in my hand I bring';
in answer to questions she expressed herself as trusting to
Jesus alone and that He was very near and precious to her.
I stood by her side holding her hand. Whenever I had to
move she gave it back to me as soon as I returned, so we
watched her for hours till the heart that was so full of love
ceased to beat, and her ransomed spirit saw the Saviour she
so longed to behold, and, with her loved ones, joined in His
praise. Often during her long illness has she said to me,
'What should I do now were it not for the Atonement of
Jesus?—when I think of the finished work of Christ I feel
no dread.'

" For months she has suffered much, but never a wish has
she expressed to have it otherwise, once she said to me,
'All my times are ordered by a loving Father, and I can
leave myself in His hands.' We thank God for all the
grace given to our beloved mother, and amidst our bitter
grief rejoice that for her the conflict is ended, and that she
is safe for ever with her husband and seven children.

" I know you will unite with us in praying that grace may
be given us to follow those who are now inheriting the
promises."

Mrs. Knibb survived her husband twenty-five years and
a half.

The circle is complete now, Mrs. Fray having entered
into rest. No, the grandsons and grand-daughters will not
say complete. They will desire to be accounted part of it.
One grandson, the Rev. Ellis Fray, has charge of Kettering,
the country station, where their affectionate people had
built the house, accepted by Mr. Knibb for Mrs. Knibb,
he being resolved to hold no property himself.

Falmouth is in the hands of Mr. Kingdon, highly
esteemed for his work's sake.

APPENDIX.

THE foregoing sketch of Mr. Knibb is so slight, considering all the subjects of interest it embraces, that the narrative has been, as much as possible, kept to him personally; but Mr. Burchell stood shoulder to shoulder with him through all the time of their service, and it is hardly possible to speak of one without the other. So it cannot be breaking the resolution of keeping to Mr. Knibb entirely, to add the following details from Mr. Burchell's papers and the diary of the Rev. Walter Dendy, kept during the troubled time of 1832, when all the missionaries were suffering more or less and the group at Montego Bay were being drawn very close together by a common bond of oppression.

Some months afterwards, when both Messrs. Knibb and Burchell were in England and present at the same drawing-room meeting, a little child, allowed to sit on a stool at her mother's feet, asked, at its close, "Why do they call each other brother, they have not the same name?" and thus got her first lesson as to brotherhood in Christ, and in this instance very special brotherhood—in trials, in interests, in aims, in works, in hopes.

Mr. Burchell arrived in Jamaica, January, 1824. He went through every possible experience there : of few hearers of the Word, then many ; of doubtful Christians with more superstition than faith, alongside of others entirely devoted to Christ ; of persecution and interminable small annoyances from many white men hating the Gospel, contrasted with the firm friendship of one or two ; of building and secular worries ; of ill-health in his own person and his

9

devoted wife lying between life and death for weeks and then recovering by a slow and trying convalescence.

Truly, by this time he had been educated up to " I can do all things through Christ that strengtheneth me."

Mr. and Mrs. Burchell had been away seven months when they arrived in Montego Bay on board the *Garland Grove*, on the 7th January, to find the town under martial law. One would have said that no ground of complaint could have been made against them. But Montego Bay was Mr. Burchell's own station. He had acquired great and deserved influence there. The opposite interest were so exasperated, that the missionaries on shore were repeatedly told, that if possible there was little doubt he (Mr. Burchell) would be assassinated. Messrs. Knibb, Abbott, and Gardiner were already detained on bail in Montego Bay.

Before coming to anchor, an officer from his Majesty's frigate *Blanche*, went on board the *Garland Grove*, and demanded of Captain Pengelly a list of his passengers.

He then required Mr. Burchell to accompany him on board the *Blanche*; simply replying to his inquiries, " It is martial law." This seizure, however painful, after a tedious voyage, was an evident interposition of Providence ; because it placed him beyond the reach of a mob, who displayed the most savage eagerness for his destruction. The detention, however, was made very disagreeable to him.

Here are extracts from Mr. Burchell's own memoranda of these anxious days :

"Saturday, 7th of January. The marine on guard walked in my apartment with his bayonet drawn; though I was not informed why I was apprehended, nor indeed that I was a prisoner. At 8 p.m. I retired to rest in a cot that was slung. The marine on guard continued during the whole night pacing to and fro in my room.

"Sunday 8th : The marine on guard still continued with his bayonet drawn, pacing the apartments I occupied.

"Monday 9th: This morning the marine paced with his bayonet sheathed. Permission was obtained for the visits of Mrs. Burchell; but it must be in the presence of a third person. About ten o'clock, a lieutenant asked me if I wished to walk on deck; after a few remarks, I signified my wish, and was then informed that a guard must accompany me.

"Tuesday 10th: The marine on guard paced the deck during the night, with his bayonet sheathed; did not enter my apartments *much;* but every half hour, when he struck the bell, came to my cot and looked upon me. An officer on watch came down several times during the night, when the bell was struck; and as far as I could understand, inquired if the prisoner was safe.

"Friday 13th: It was required that all Mr. Burchell's papers should be sent to the Custos.

"17th: Suffering from the confinement, begged to go on deck for fresh air.

"18th: Removed from the *Blanche* to the *Garland Grove.* During the eleven days I have been kept a prisoner on board the *Blanche* frigate, I have received no information of the reason of my apprehension and imprisonment, though during this period I have been deprived of all intercourse with any person but Mrs. Burchell. I have been permitted to go on deck but twice."

Years after Mrs. Burchell herself told the tale of that first interview "in the presence of a third person." She was in fearful anxiety and had begged hard in several quarters to be allowed to see her husband, before this conditional leave was obtained. It did not reassure her while she was waiting for admittance to overhear some one say he was sorry for Mrs. Burchell and the child. At last a young officer came to conduct her to the cabin; when she had entered he said, "I am the person appointed to be present at your interview," then turned away, went out of the cabin and locked the door. She enrolled him in her memory as one of her best friends

On Friday, January the 20th, Mr. Burchell having been returned to the *Garland Grove*, where Mr. Manderson and Mr. Delisser visited him, he notes, "I asked Mr. Manderson what was the cause of my apprehension, and if he would inform me what charge there was against me ;. he replied that there was no charge at present, and that Mr. Custos Barrett, who was examining my papers, had informed him that hitherto he had found nothing which in the least implicated me, nor which one planter could not write to another."

On the same day, and the next, Mr. Burchell was visited by some of the missionaries from the shore, but, as Captain Pengelly got into trouble for this permission, it was not repeated.

In this situation—a prisoner for an unknown cause—Mr. Burchell continued till February 10th, when Captain Pengelly received from Mr. Custos Barrett the following official document* :—

"MONTEGO BAY,

"10th *February*, 1832.

"SIR,—You are hereby authorised to release from detention the person of Mr. Burchell.

(Signed)   "RICHARD BARRETT, Custos.

"To Captain PENGELLY, Ship *Garland Grove*."

Captain Pengelly called at once on the missionaries on

---

* An extract from Mr. Dendy's journal throws some light on the effort to obtain evidence :—"Feb. 7-8.— . . . was introduced to a Miss ——— who had been confined many hours with a view to eliciting evidence against Mr. Burchell. She had been taken to a window of the Court-house and shown the gallows, and threatened to be hung if she did not acknowledge that Mr. Burchell had sent her three letters to be read to the negroes to tell them to be free. She replied she would not tell a lie, and that it would have been no use for Mr. Burchell to send her letters for she could not have read them——"

Thos. Birchell

shore, and urged that Mr. Burchell's life would be in danger if he landed, and that he should go away to America for a season, an American vessel being in the harbour which would take him on board. While this was under consideration, a boat came alongside the *Garland Grove* with a fresh warrant of arrest. The officer in charge was to take him on shore ; he assured them that Mr. Burchell's person would be safe in his charge. The landing, however, was into the midst of an angry mob, and, in all probability, Mr. Burchell owed his life to a company of the coloured militia who volunteered as an escort.

Mr. Gardiner was associated with him in this second imprisonment. They were committed on the evidence of a slave named Stennett. This poor man's conscience made him so miserable that he shortly afterwards confessed that he had been bribed to give the evidence he did, and although he was abused and threatened he could not be shaken from his purpose, but persisted that his present recantation, and not the former affidavit, expressed the real truth. To the very faces of the persons who had persuaded and bribed him, he boldly said : " You know you did, and you cannot deny it. And you, Mr. Delisser, Mr. Morris, and Mr. Bowen, were the first who spoke to me about it, and offered me money if I would do it." This was the 11th of February, but these prisoners (Messrs. Burchell and Gardiner) were not released.

On the 3rd of March their legal adviser, Mr. James Forsyth, arrived from Kingston. In him they found not only an intelligent, zealous agent, but a pious, fervent disciple of their common Lord. He was determined to use his utmost ability to overcome the enemy.

In the meantime, the chapel at Montego Bay had been destroyed by a lawless mob, and an attack was threatened on the persons and lodgings of the missionaries on shore. As it was considered dangerous to remain on shore for the night, Mr. Roby obtained a somewhat unwilling permission for them to go on board a king's ship in the harbour. The officers of the wardroom received them kindly, but early the next morning the captain sent them a message that they must prepare to go on shore; in the end they were allowed to wait till Mr. Roby came on board. It was understood that the feeling on shore had considerably subsided except towards Mr. Knibb, whom the captain of the *North Star* was persuaded to retain for another night, while Messrs. Whitehorne, Abbott, and Gardiner returned to their lodgings.

Mr. Roby had obtained through his kindness to the missionaries so much ill-will from the populace that they hung him in effigy in the market-place. The lay figure used for the purpose is said to have been made in the first instance for Mr. Burchell.

In a pecuniary point of view, Mr. Burchell was the greatest loser of all the missionaries. Not only was his chapel ruined, but his own house, which was his private property (he having resources of his own), was destroyed.

He left for the United States on being set free from bail, on the advice of some of his non-missionary friends.

The two friends, or "brothers" in Christ, were not long divided by death. Mr. Burchell followed Mr. Knibb on the 15th May, 1846, surviving him only six months.

ALEXANDER & SHEPHEARD, 27, Chancery Lane, London, W.C.

Lightning Source UK Ltd.
Milton Keynes UK
UKHW020657120520
363107UK00010B/2934